SAMS
Teach Yourself
MICROSOFT®
OUTLOOK® 2000

Joe Habraken

in 10 Minutes

SAMS

201 West 103rd St., Indianapolis, Indiana, 46290 USA

SAMS TEACH YOURSELF MICROSOFT® OUTLOOK® 2000 IN 10 MINUTES

Copyright © 1999 by Sams Publishing

International Standard Book Number: 0-672-31450-9

Library of Congress Catalog Card Number: 98-87073

Printed in the United States of America

First Printing: May 1999

00   99   4   3   2

TRADEMARKS

WARNING AND DISCLAIMER

EXECUTIVE EDITOR
Mark Taber

ACQUISITIONS EDITOR
Randi Roger

DEVELOPMENT EDITOR
Scott D. Meyers

MANAGING EDITOR
Lisa Wilson

PROJECT EDITOR
Rebecca Mounts

COPY EDITORS
Kim Cofer
Tonya Maddox
Suzanne Rose
Maryann Steinhart

INDEXER
Aamir Burki

PROOFREADER
Kim Cofer

TECHNICAL EDITOR
Sunil Hazari

INTERIOR DESIGN
Gary Adair

COVER DESIGN
Aren Howell

LAYOUT TECHNICIANS
Staci Somers
Mark Walchle

CONTENTS

ABOUT THE AUTHOR

Joe Habraken is a computer technology professional and author with more than 12 years of experience as an educator and consultant in the information technology field. Joe is a Microsoft Certified Professional and has taught computer software seminars across the country. He has a Masters degree from the American University in Washington, D.C. and currently serves as the lead instructor for the Networking Technologies program at Globe College in St. Paul, MN. Joe's recent book titles include *The Microsoft Access 97 Exam Guide, Microsoft Office 2000 6 in 1,* and *Using Lotus SmartSuite Millennium Edition.*

DEDICATION

To my incredible niece, Lena, who makes the outlook for the future seem very bright!

ACKNOWLEDGMENTS

Creating books like this takes a real team effort. I would like to thank Randi Roger, our Acquisitions Editor, who worked very hard to assemble the team that made this book a reality. I would also like to thank Scott Meyers, who served as the Development Editor for this book and who came up with many great ideas for improving the content of the book. Also a tip of the hat and a thanks to Sunil Hazari, who as the Technical Editor for the project did a fantastic job making sure that everything was accurate and suggested a number of additions that made the book even more technically sound. Finally, a great big thanks to our Project Editor, Rebecca Mounts, who ran the last leg of the race and made sure the book made it to press on time—what a great team of professionals

TELL US WHAT YOU THINK!

As the reader of this book, *you* are our most important critic and commentator. We value your opinion and want to know what we're doing right, what we could do better, what areas you'd like to see us publish in, and any other words of wisdom you're willing to pass our way.

You can fax, email, or write me directly to let me know what you did or didn't like about this book—as well as what we can do to make our books stronger.

Please note that I cannot help you with technical problems related to the topic of this book, and that due to the high volume of mail I receive, I might not be able to reply to every message.

When you write, please be sure to include this book's title and author as well as your name and phone or fax number. I will carefully review your comments and share them with the author and editors who worked on the book.

Fax: 317-581-4770

Email: office_sams@mcp.com

Mail: Mark Taber
         Associate Publisher
         Sams Publishing
         201 West 103rd Street
         Indianapolis, IN 46290 USA

INTRODUCTION

Microsoft Outlook is a personal information manager (PIM). With Outlook, you can communicate throughout your office or over the Internet with email. You can also schedule meetings, create task lists for yourself and others, store documents in public folders, and launch Internet applications such as Microsoft Internet Explorer and Microsoft NetMeeting. Outlook provides accessibility and flexibility for you and your co-workers and friends.

THE WHAT AND WHY OF MICROSOFT OUTLOOK

Outlook can help you organize your work on a day-to-day basis. Using Microsoft Outlook, you can do the following:

- Create task lists

- Manage your calendar

- Log phone calls and other important events in your journal

- Make notes to remind yourself of important tasks

Additionally, Outlook can help you communicate with others and share your workload. When you and your co-workers use the combined features of Microsoft Outlook and Microsoft Office, you can

- Schedule meetings and invite co-workers

- Communicate with others using email

- Import and export files

- Share data and documents through public folders

- Communicate with others over the Internet

Microsoft Outlook is easy to learn and offers many advantages and benefits in return. This book can help you understand the possibilities awaiting you with Microsoft Outlook.

This book concentrates on using Outlook on a Windows 98 workstation on which Microsoft Office is also installed. Note, however, that you can also install Microsoft Outlook on a computer running Windows NT 4.0.

WHY *Sams Teach Yourself Yourself Microsoft Outlook 2000 in 10 Minutes?*

Sams Teach Yourself Microsoft Outlook 2000 in 10 Minutes can save you precious time while you get to know the program. Each lesson is designed to be completed in 10 minutes or less, so you'll be up to snuff in basic Outlook skills quickly.

Although you can jump around among lessons, starting at the beginning is a good plan. The bare-bones basics are covered first, and more advanced topics are covered later. If you need help installing Outlook, see the next section for instructions.

INSTALLING OUTLOOK

You can install Microsoft Outlook to a workstation running Windows 95, Windows 98, or Windows NT 4.0. (Outlook will *not* run on a computer running Windows for Workgroups, Windows 3.x, or Windows NT 3.5.) In addition, you can install Outlook in conjunction with Microsoft Office 97, or you can install just the Outlook program.

To install Outlook, follow these steps:

1. Start your computer and insert the Microsoft Office CD-ROM in the CD-ROM drive.

2. Choose Start, Run. Alternatively, open the CD-ROM and choose the Setup icon.

3. In the Run dialog box, type the letter of the CD-ROM drive and follow it with **setup** (for example, *e:\setup*). If necessary, use the Browse button to locate and select the CD-ROM drive and the setup.exe program.

4. When Setup prompts you, enter your name and organization. Confirm that they are correct.

5. Choose either the Upgrade Now or the Custom option.

6. Follow the onscreen instructions to complete the installation.

The new Microsoft Installation Interface lists an icon for each of the Office products available on your CD-ROM, such as Outlook. A plus symbol next to a particular software application enables you to open and view all the components for that application. You have the option of clicking a particular component and then choosing from a menu how you want the component installed: Run From My Computer (meaning it is installed on your PC); Run From CD (the component is run from CD, so make sure you keep it in the CD-ROM drive); and Installed on First Use (the component is not installed from the CD until you use the component for the first time).

After you complete the installation from the CD, you are ready to run your Office applications.

When you start Outlook for the first time on your computer you will be asked if you want to configure Outlook for Internet E-mail Only or Corporate E-mail (a third choice is available for no email). Lesson 3, "Understanding the Outlook Configurations," discusses the effect that these two different configurations have on Outlook functionality. You may want to review Lesson 3 briefly before selecting your installation.

Microsoft also offers software upgrades via their Web site. You can download updates and fixes for Outlook and the other Microsoft Office applications. Go to **http://www.microsoft.com/Office**. Use the search feature on this page to locate additional information and updates related to Outlook.

CONVENTIONS USED IN THIS BOOK

To help you move through the lessons easily, these conventions are used:

Onscreen text	Onscreen text appears in bold type.
Text you type	Information you need to type appears in bold blue type.
Items you select	Commands, options, and icons you select and keys you press appear in colored type.

In telling you to choose menu commands, this book uses the format *menu title, menu command*. For example, "Choose File, Properties" means you should "open the File menu and select the Properties command."

In addition to those conventions, *Sams Teach Yourself Microsoft Outlook 2000 in 10 Minutes* uses the following icons to identify helpful information:

 Plain English   New or unfamiliar terms are defined in (you got it) "plain English."

 Timesaver Tips   Read these tips for ideas that cut corners and confusion.

 Panic Button   This icon identifies areas where new users often run into trouble; these tips offer practical solutions to those problems.

LESSON 1
WHAT'S NEW IN OUTLOOK 2000

In this lesson you are introduced to Outlook's powerful organizing features, and you learn what's new in Outlook 2000.

GETTING ORGANIZED WITH OUTLOOK 2000

Outlook 2000 is the latest version of Microsoft's popular personal information manager (PIM). Outlook can help you manage incoming and outgoing messages, such as email and faxes, and help you keep organized by providing a personal calendar, a contacts list, and a personal to-do list.

 Personal Information Manager (PIM) A PIM is a software package that helps you keep track of your appointments, meetings, contacts, and messages, such as email and faxes.

Outlook 2000 shows a number of improvements over previous versions of the software. It is closely integrated with Internet Explorer 5, Microsoft NetMeeting, and the other applications found in Microsoft Office 2000.

For instance, Outlook provides easy access to your Internet Explorer 5 browser for viewing Web pages. Outlook also enables you to easily schedule online meetings using the Contact feature and then hold the meeting using the Microsoft NetMeeting software. If you read or post to newsgroups on the Internet, Outlook enables you to access Usenet groups using the Outlook Express newsreading tools. (See Lesson 26, "Outlook 2000 and the Internet," for more about Outlook and its integration with Microsoft Web and Internet tools.)

Outlook also is tightly integrated with the other applications in Microsoft Office 2000, such as Microsoft Word and Microsoft Excel. You can choose to use Microsoft Word as your email editor, enabling you to use all the features in Word to compose your messages. You also can easily include files created in the other Office components in any of the items that you create in Outlook (mail messages, Calendar events, and so on). For instance, you can embed an Excel worksheet in an Outlook appointment on the Calendar. That way when you have to get to that important meeting on time, you have your Excel worksheet with the meeting data right at your fingertips.

 Version Replacement Be aware that when you install Outlook 2000, it replaces the current version of Outlook you have installed on your computer (this includes Outlook 97 and 98). The Outlook 2000 installation also affects your Outlook Express version. Outlook Express 5 (the version that ships with Internet Explorer 5) replaces the current version. This is because Outlook uses Outlook Express as its default Newsgroup client.

UNDERSTANDING OUTLOOK'S FOLDERS

If you are new to Outlook you will find that it provides an environment similar to a filing cabinet. Items of information are kept in folders, which you can access with one click of the mouse. These folders are accessed from the Outlook bar that appears on the left side of the Outlook window (see Figure 1.1). To open a folder, just click on it.

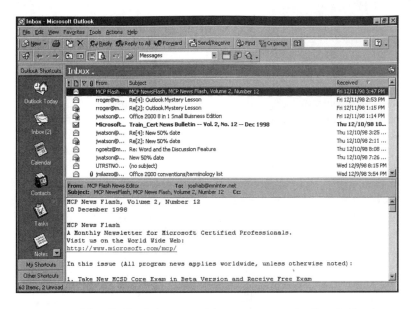

FIGURE 1.1   The Outlook bar provides easy access to the Outlook folders, such as the Inbox and Calendar.

For instance, your new email and fax messages can be found in the Inbox. Appointments, meetings, and events are stored in the Calendar folder. Contacts—their email addresses, business addresses, fax numbers, and phone numbers—are stored in the Contacts folder.

Folders are available for your Tasks, Journal entries, and Notes. Outlook also keeps track of your Deleted Items and Sent Items in folders. Outlook 2000 also has a feature called Net Folders, which enable you to share Outlook information with others over the Internet or a corporate intranet. Any Outlook item, such as a message, a task, or an appointment, can be shared using these special folders.

All these various folders are covered in this book. For a quick overview of navigating the Outlook window, check out Lesson 4, "Using Outlook's Tools."

NEW FEATURES IN OUTLOOK 2000

Users of previous versions of Outlook will discover that Outlook 2000 contains a number of improvements that make it easier for you to access and update the information in your various folders. New features have also been added that make Outlook 2000 even more user friendly than earlier versions of this powerful personal information manager.

THE PERSONALIZED MENU AND TOOLBAR SYSTEM

As with all of Office 2000, Outlook 2000 has adopted a new menu system that enables easy access to the commands that you use most often. When you first choose a particular menu, you will find a short list of menu commands. As you use additional commands, Outlook automatically adds them to your menu list.

You can turn off the personalized menu system if you want, which enables you to see all the commands available on each menu. Follow these steps:

1. Click the Tools menu, then click Customize. The Customize dialog box appears.

2. Click the Options tab of the dialog box (see Figure 1.2).

FIGURE 1.2   You can turn off the personalized menu system in the Customize dialog box.

You will find that this "personalized" strategy is also embraced by the toolbar system. As you use commands, they are added to the toolbar. This provides you with customized menus and toolbars that are, in effect, personalized for you.

THE OUTLOOK HELP SYSTEM

The Outlook help system now has a very different look when compared to previous versions. Even the Office Assistant has cast aside its Assistant's box and now resides directly on the Windows desktop.

Additionally, the Office Assistant is more intuitive than ever. For example, when the Assistant displays a light bulb over its head, clicking the Assistant will often present you with helpful advice on the feature or action with which you are currently working.

If you have limited screen space or you just don't like the Office Assistant, you can easily turn off this help feature. Just clear the Use Office Assistant check box in the Assistant's Option dialog box (right-click on the Assistant and then select Options from the shortcut menu). If you then find yourself in need of help, you can access the help system from the Help menu on the Outlook menu bar.

The new Outlook help system provides you with an environment that is similar to what you find in a Web browser. Help topics are represented as hyperlinks, and Back and Forward buttons make it easy for you to move backward and forward through the help screens that you have accessed (see Figure 1.3).

 The New Help System is Available Through the Assistant Even if you use the Office Assistant to get help, once you click one of the Assistant's answers to your help query you are taken to the help window described in this section.

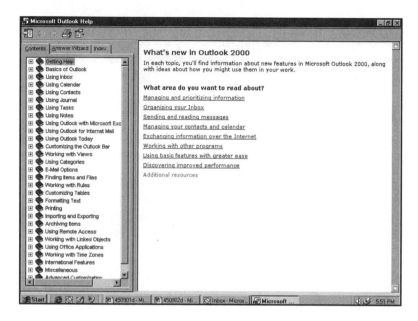

Figure 1.3   The new help system provides you with an easy-to-use environment.

The new help system also contains an Answer Wizard that can answer specific questions. The Answer Wizard tab, along with the Contents tab and Index tab, provide you with a set of powerful choices for getting help in Outlook. For more about using the help system and the Office Assistant, see Lesson 4.

OTHER NEW FEATURES

Outlook 2000 has improved many of the features introduced in Outlook 98. Additionally, a number of other new features that enhance the "usability" of Outlook have been added to this version.

For instance, Outlook will now warn you if you are duplicating an entry for a currently existing contact in your Contacts folder. You are given the option of merging any new data that you have created in the duplicate contact record with the information in the already existing contact record.

Outlook's integration with the Web also has been enhanced in this version. You can now publish your Calendar as a Web page, easily converting the information in it to HTML. Other Web-ready improvements include better integration of Microsoft NetMeeting and integration of Microsoft Netshow with Outlook.

OTHER FEATURES YOU SHOULD BE AWARE OF

If you are new to Outlook, some features may seem somewhat confusing to you on first inspection. This section discusses some of the more complex features in Outlook and how they impact your use of the software.

THE OUTLOOK SETUP WIZARD

While the Setup Wizard is not new with this version of Outlook, you should be aware that the Outlook Setup Wizard gives you the option of configuring Outlook for either a Corporate or an Internet E-mail Only account. The type of configuration you choose during installation will affect which of the fax services, Microsoft Fax or WinFax, is available to you for sending and receiving faxes.

The Setup Wizard also can import existing email accounts from other email clients such as Outlook Express, Netscape Messenger, or Eudora Mail. If you've used a previous version of Outlook, the Setup Wizard also can import existing accounts, profiles, folders, and personal address books.

 Connection Choices   The Internet Only selection means that you send and receive email over the Internet by connecting with a modem to an Internet service provider. If you are connected to a corporate network or if you dial in to a corporate network using your modem, the best choice for you is the Corporate or Workgroup setting. This selection still enables you to send Internet email.

What If I Use America Online?   If you use America Online, you will not be able to use Outlook as your email client. However, you can still use all the other features that Outlook offers. You may want to install Outlook without email support.

THE RULES WIZARD AND ORGANIZER TOOL

The Rules Wizard and Organizer tool are two features that help you create rules (also known as filters in some email programs) that can forward, move, delete, or flag incoming and outgoing email. For instance, you may want all email from a certain sender to be transferred to a special folder. Important email that you want to forward to other individuals also can be handled automatically.

Rules created using the Rules Wizard can be based on the sender of the message or the content of the message. You can create a rule that categorizes messages with a certain content. Or you can flag messages received from a particular person.

The Organizer tool provides an easy-to-use interface that enables you to quickly organize your message using folders, colors, flags, and special views. It also helps you create simple rules to organize messages from a particular person. Most importantly, it can help you create rules that quickly deal with nuisance messages that you consider junk mail.

OUTLOOK AND INTERNET EXPLORER 5

As mentioned earlier, Outlook 2000 is seamlessly integrated with the components of Microsoft's Internet Explorer 5 so that you can quickly access an important World Wide Web page, read Usenet newsgroup postings, or launch an online meeting using Microsoft NetMeeting. Outlook also can be configured as your default email client so that it opens when you click a Web page email link in the Internet Explorer window.

When Outlook 2000 is installed, Internet Explorer 5 and the Outlook Express NewsReader are also installed. Microsoft NetMeeting can be downloaded as an addition to your Internet Explorer from the NetMeeting Web page at **http://www.microsoft.com/netmeeting/**.

Exploring Outlook Features   This book gives you a chance to explore each of the Outlook 2000 features discussed in this lesson.

In this lesson you learned how Outlook can help you stay organized. You were also introduced to some of the new features found in Outlook 2000. In the next lesson you take a first look at the Outlook window and learn how to start and exit the software. You also learn how to use the mouse to navigate through the various features of the program.

LESSON 2

GETTING STARTED WITH OUTLOOK

In this lesson you learn to start and exit Outlook, identify parts of the Outlook window, and use the mouse to get around the program.

STARTING OUTLOOK

You start Outlook from the Windows desktop. After starting the program, you can leave it open, or you can minimize it to free up the desktop for other applications. Either way, you can access it at any time during your workday.

 Outlook and System Performance If you leave Outlook open on your desktop, it will still require a certain amount of your system resources. This means that if you normally run multiple applications such as Word and Excel, you may see some loss of performance as you work. If this becomes a problem, close Outlook to free up your system's memory. Adding memory to your system, of course, is also an alternative for increasing performance.

To start Microsoft Outlook, follow these steps:

1. From the Windows desktop, click the Start button and choose Programs, Microsoft Outlook. You can also double-click the Outlook shortcut icon on the desktop to start Outlook, or you can click the Outlook icon on the Quick Launch toolbar on the Windows 98 taskbar.

2. If the Choose Profile dialog box appears, click OK to accept the default profile or choose your profile and open Microsoft Outlook. Figure 2.1 shows the Outlook screen that appears.

 Use the Office Toolbar You can also launch Outlook from the Office toolbar if it is present on your desktop. Click the Office menu button to add the Outlook button to the Office toolbar.

 Profile Information about you and your communication services that is created automatically when you install Outlook. Profiles are related to the Corporate Installation of Outlook. The profile includes your name, user ID, post office, and so on. Additional profiles allow you to set up Outlook for more than one user or a different set of communication services. Configuration issues regarding Outlook and Internet Only and Corporate email will be addressed in more detail in Lesson 3, "Understanding the Outlook Configurations."

Outlook bar   Click here to show Folder list   Restore button

Title bar| Menu bar   Toolbar   Minimize button |Close button

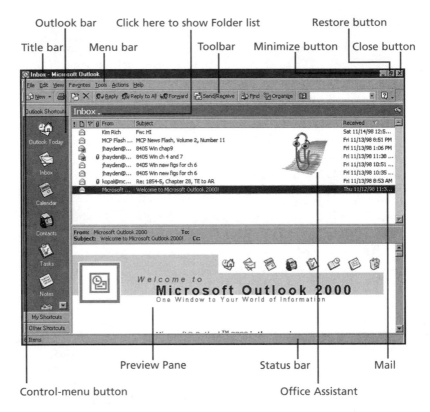

Control-menu button   Preview Pane   Status bar   Mail

Office Assistant

Figure 2.1 The Outlook window includes many icons and items you'll use in your daily routine.

UNDERSTANDING THE OUTLOOK WINDOW

The Outlook Window includes items you can use to navigate and operate the program. If you do not see some of the items listed in Figure 2.1 on your screen, open the View menu and select the command for the appropriate element (such as Toolbars, Status Bar, Folder List, or Outlook Bar). A check mark in front of an item means the item is currently showing.

Close the Preview Pane   If you find the Preview Pane distracting when you first open the Outlook Window, click the View menu and click Preview Pane to close the Preview Pane.

Table 2.1 describes the elements you see in the opening screen.

TABLE 2.1   ELEMENTS OF THE OUTLOOK WINDOW

ELEMENT	DESCRIPTION
Title bar	Includes the name of the application and current folder, plus the Minimize, Maximize, and Close buttons.
Control menu button	Opens the Control menu, which provides such commands as Move, Size, Minimize, and Close.
Minimize button	Reduces the Outlook window to a button on the taskbar; to restore the window to its original size, click the button on the taskbar.
Maximize button	Enlarges the Outlook window to cover the Windows 95 desktop. When the window is maximized, the Maximize button changes to a Restore button that you can click to return the window to its previous size.
Close (X) button	Closes the Outlook program window.
Menu bar	Contains menus of commands you can use to perform tasks in the program.
Toolbar	Includes icons that serve as shortcuts for common commands, such as creating a new message or printing a message.

continues

TABLE 2.1   CONTINUED

ELEMENT	DESCRIPTION
Show Folder list	Displays the current folder. Click this to display a list of Personal Folders you can open.
Outlook bar	Displays icons representing folders: Inbox, Calendar, Contacts, and so on. Click an icon to change to the folder it names. The Outlook, Mail, and Other buttons on the bar list specific groups of folders (for instance, the Mail button lists icons related to your mail, such as the Inbox and Sent items).
Status bar	Displays information about the items currently shown in the Information Viewer.
Preview Pane	Displays a preview of the currently selected item in your Outlook Inbox or other selected folder.
Office Assistant	The Office Assistant provides you with the help you need to get the most out of Outlook. Click the Assistant when you need help.

 Finding a Toolbar Button's Purpose   You can place the mouse pointer on any toolbar button to view a description of that tool's function.

USING THE MOUSE IN OUTLOOK

As with most Windows-based programs, you can use the mouse in Outlook to select items, open mail and folders, move items, and so on. In general, clicking selects an item, and double-clicking selects it and performs some action on it (for example, displaying its contents).

- In addition to clicking and double-clicking, there are some special mouse actions you can use in Outlook. First, to move an object to another position on the screen (to transfer a mail message to another folder, for example), you can *drag* the object with the mouse. To drag an object to a new location onscreen, point to the object and press and hold down the left mouse button. Move the mouse pointer to the new location, and then release the mouse button.

- As another example, you can display a shortcut menu by clicking the right mouse button when pointing to an item. For instance, you can right-click a folder in the Outlook bar or a piece of mail. A shortcut menu appears, which usually contains common commands relating to that particular item.

- Finally, you can act upon multiple items at once by selecting them before issuing a command. To select multiple contiguous items, hold down the Shift key and click the first and last items you want to select. To select noncontiguous items (those that are not adjacent to each other), hold down the Ctrl key and click each item.

 If You Prefer the Keyboard   You can use the keyboard to move around Outlook and to access many, but not all, of its features. For example, to open a menu with the keyboard, press the Alt key and then press the underlined letter in the menu name (press Alt+F to open the File menu, for instance). This book concentrates on using the mouse to perform tasks in Outlook; however, some keyboard shortcuts are included in tips along the way.

EXITING OUTLOOK

When you're finished with Outlook, you can close the program in several different ways:

- Choose File, Exit (to remain connected to the mail program).

- Choose File, Exit and Log Off (to disconnect from the mail program).

- Double-click the application's Control-menu button.

- Click the application's Control-menu button and choose Close from the menu.

- Press Alt+F4.

- Click the Close (X) button at the right end of Outlook's title bar.

DO I NEED TO LOG OFF?

If you are connected to your email service through your corporate network, you really do not need to log off or close Outlook. This allows Outlook to periodically check the mail server for new mail. When you log off your corporate network and close down your computer, your connection to the mail server is also shut down. New email will wait for you on the server and be downloaded the next time you log on to the network and start Outlook.

If you send or receive your email through a mail server run by an Internet service provider, you connect through a dial-up connection. After you upload or download your email from the server using Outlook, you may want to disconnect from your provider to save on connection time or to free up your phone line. Figure 2.2 shows the connection box used for a dial-up service. To close the connection, click Disconnect.

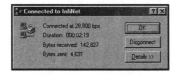

Figure 2.2 After downloading your email from your Internet service provider, you may want to close the connection.

In this lesson you learned about the Outlook window, how to start and exit Outlook, and how to use the mouse to get around the program. In the next lesson, you learn to open menus, select commands, and use dialog boxes and the toolbar.

Lesson 3

Understanding the Outlook Configurations

In this lesson you learn how to set up Outlook for Internet Only or Corporate email and how to configure these two different options.

Choosing Your Outlook Installation

The choices that you make during Outlook's initial installation will affect the functionality of the Outlook software and the features that are available to you. However, don't be overly concerned with the preceding statement; you can reinstall components of Outlook at any time or change your installation depending on your needs.

Outlook 2000 really comes in two flavors: Internet Only and Corporate (or WorkGroup) email service (actually a third installation option allows you to install Outlook with no electronic mail support). Which configuration you choose revolves around whether you are connected to a corporate network or using Outlook as your Internet email client. Each installation also has certain ways of handling the sending and receiving of messages, the handling of faxes, and how collaboration with other users is conducted.

INSTALLATION CONSIDERATIONS

When you begin the Outlook 2000 installation, you should be aware that any previous version of Outlook will be replaced. Another inescapable result of the Outlook 2000 installation is that Internet Explorer 5 (or later version) will be installed replacing any previous versions of Microsoft Internet Explorer that you have on your computer. You don't have to use Internet Explorer 5 as your default Web browser, but it must be installed on the computer for Outlook to have full functionality.

The only major installation decision that you must make is whether you want Internet Only email, Corporate email, or No email at all, as shown in Figure 3.1. The following sections look at the first two possibilities separately.

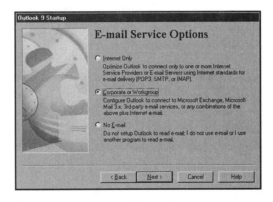

FIGURE 3.1   You must select the type of electronic mail you will use with Outlook.

INTERNET ONLY EMAIL

If you select Internet Only email you probably connect to the Internet using a modem and an Internet Service Provider (ISP). Your ISP has supplied you with a typical Internet email account that uses Internet communication protocols like POP3, IMAP, and SMTP. You use Outlook as your Internet email client to send and receive messages using your account.

The other reason that you may choose Internet Only email is in cases where you are physically connected to a network at your place of business, but your company does not operate a special network mail server with Microsoft Exchange Server software installed on it or another corporate email server software package installed on it. And so your company uses Internet email for its corporate communications. Again, you are taking advantage of Outlook's ability to manage your email account and send and receive standard Internet email.

ISP (Internet Service Provider)   A commercial, educational, or government institution that provides individuals and companies access to the Internet.

POP3 (Post Office Protocol version 3)   A set of rules used to download mail to your computer. Your ISP uses a POP3 host, or server, to get your mail to you.

SMTP (Simple Mail Transfer Protocol)   A set of rules used to transfer Internet mail; your ISP goes through an SMTP host, or relay, server to get your mail to you.

IMAP (Internet Message Access Protocol)   A set of software rules used by an email client to access email messages on a shared mail server as if the messages were stored locally.

The only features in Outlook that will be affected by your selection of Internet Only email will be your mail service and your fax service. The Calendar, Contacts, Notes, and Tasks features will operate the same. However, the way that you share Calendar and Contacts information with other users will be different than it would be on a corporate network using Exchange Server.

One other point concerning the two different email configurations in Outlook is the different formats that are available to you for sending mail. The Internet Only configuration allows you to send messages as Text Only and Rich Text (HTML). The Rich Text (HTML) format for the Internet Only configuration is really just HTML, so do not be confused by the Rich Text reference. When you send HTML messages, you can use special fonts, bold, underline, and other font attributes. If the person receiving the message has an email client that can read HTML, that person will see your special formatting.

The Corporate configuration provides you with the Text Only format and the Rich Text (HTML) format and adds a third format, Rich Text Format (RTF). This Rich Text Format is normally used for messages sent locally on your corporate network. Local mail networks at a company usually employ the same email client, and so each user can take advantage of this RTF format. This RTF format differs from the RTF (HTML) format because it is particular to proprietary email packages such as Microsoft Mail and was not really designed to be used for messages sent over the Internet. The term Rich Text really refers (in both the HTML and Rich Text formats) to the fact that the text in the message can be formatted using special text attributes such as bold, underline, and italic.

CONFIGURING AN INTERNET EMAIL ACCOUNT

When you start Outlook for the first time after the installation in which you chose Internet Only, you will be asked to configure your Internet email account. If your previous version of Outlook (or other Internet email client, such as Outlook Express) was configured for an Internet email account, this information is imported into Outlook 98 during the installation process (a screen during preinstallation asks you to select the email client that you want to import the information from).

If no previous configuration exists, the Internet Connection Wizard will walk you through the process of creating an Internet email account as shown in Figure 3.2.

 Install It Any Time   You can install your Internet email account at any time using the Connection Wizard. Click Tools, Accounts. In the Accounts dialog box's Mail tab, click Add, and then select Mail.

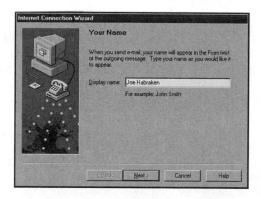

FIGURE 3.2   The Internet Connection Wizard helps you configure your Internet email account.

The Internet Connection Wizard will ask you to provide your name, your Internet email account address (probably **yourname@company.com**), and the names of your POP3 or IMAP Server (for incoming mail) and your SMTP Server (for outgoing mail). You need to get this information from your ISP or Network Administrator.

You will also be asked your POP account name and password. This information, again, must be provided to you by your ISP or Network Administrator.

The Internet Connection Wizard will also ask you to provide a "friendly" name for the account you are creating. This is the name that will appear in the Outlook Services box.

The final step in the Internet email configuration is to select the way that you will connect to the Internet. You can connect using your phone line (Outlook will help you make the connection each time you send mail), or connect using your corporate network as shown in Figure 3.3. A third choice is available if you want to manually connect to the Internet before attempting to send or receive mail using Outlook.

The final step in the process asks you to select an existing dial-up connection or create a new one to connect to the Internet (if you chose the Connect Using Your Phone Line option in the previous step).

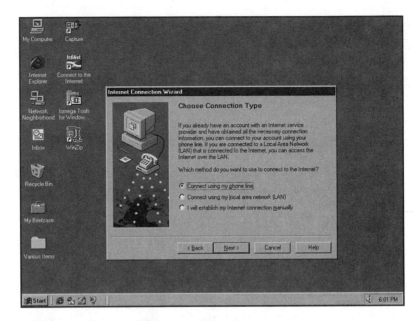

FIGURE 3.3   Choose how you will connect to the Internet when you send and receive messages using your email account.

Dial-up connections dial the phone number of your service provider and connect you to their Internet server using your modem. If you configure a new dial-up connection, you must know your username, password, and the phone number for your ISP's Internet server.

Dial-Up Networking   You must have the Windows 98/95 or NT Dial-Up Networking protocol installed to create new dial-up connections. See your operating system documentation to learn how to configure the Windows dial-up adapter.

After you configure your Internet email account, you are ready to send and receive messages.

CONFIGURING INTERNET ONLY FAX SUPPORT

Outlook also allows you to send and receive faxes. If you configure Outlook for Internet Only and choose to send and receive faxes, Semantics' WinFax Basic version will be installed. WinFax can send faxes over your modem and answer your phone to receive incoming faxes.

The WinFax service is automatically installed during the initial installation of Outlook (if you choose Internet Only fax support during installation) and will appear as one of the accounts in the Accounts dialog box. Sending and receiving faxes in Outlook is discussed in Lesson 25, "Managing Faxes with Outlook."

SHARING INFORMATION ON THE INTERNET

Even if you are not connected to a corporate network that uses Microsoft Exchange Server to share Outlook folder information, you can share your Calendar and Contacts information with others by means of the Internet. Outlook 2000 contains a feature called Net Folders. These special folders allow you to share information on the Internet with anyone you can send Internet email to. Net Folders are discussed in Lesson 26, "Outlook 2000 and the Internet."

CORPORATE EMAIL

If you select the Corporate email configuration for Outlook during the installation process, chances are that you will be using Outlook as a corporate email client over your company's network. If your company has a Microsoft Exchange server on the network, you will be using Outlook in an ideal environment. However, even if Exchange server is not used at your company, you will find that Outlook has been designed to work with other proprietary email systems such as Lotus cc:Mail.

CONFIGURING YOUR EMAIL ACCOUNT

If you use corporate email, your network administrator will provide you with a mail account. You may or may not be allowed to choose your own username and password for the account. Your corporate email account will be configured as an account that appears in the Account dialog box. Using the Corporate email configuration allows you to take advantage of

Outlook features such as the message recall, where you can recall a mail message that has not been opened by the recipient.

If you also want to send and receive Internet email using the corporate configuration, you must create an Internet email account. You can do this adding Internet email as a service.

To add an Internet email account to the Corporate Outlook installation, select Tools, Services. In the Services dialog box, click the Add button. The Add Service to Profile dialog box appears. (See Figure 3.4.) Click Internet E-mail on the list of services and then click OK. The Mail Account Properties dialog box appears. Provide the necessary account information and also provide the names of the POP3 and SMTP servers on the Server tab (these names are usually the same because most ISPs use one server to handle POP and SMTP). After you have provided all the necessary information, click OK.

The new Internet E-mail account will be added to the list of services. Click OK to close the Services dialog box. Outlook opens a message box to let you know that the new service will not be available until you close Outlook and then restart it.

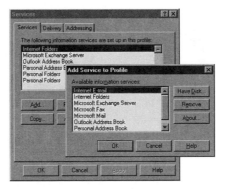

FIGURE 3.4   You can add an Internet email account to the Corporate Outlook configuration.

SHARING INFORMATION

Working on a corporate network that uses Exchange Server enables you to publish contact lists or calendars to a Microsoft Exchange Server public folder. Collaboration is made easy in the Exchange Server environment, and when you use Outlook to schedule a meeting, the availability of all the participants can be checked and routed to you immediately. A number of third-party collaboration applications also exist, making the Exchange Server environment ideal for employees using Outlook as their collaboration client.

Using Outlook on an Exchange Server network enables a number of email features not available in the Internet Only email configuration. On a network, you can redirect replies, set message expirations, and even grant privileges to other users to monitor your email, calendar, contacts, and tasks.

Working on a corporate network also enhances your ability to share information between users. Any folder on your computer can be set up as a shared resource. Shared folders can serve as discussion folders, where individuals on the corporate network can post and read messages (see Figure 3.5).

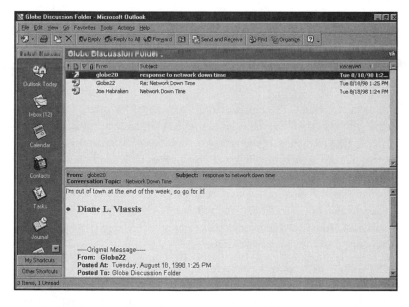

FIGURE 3.5   Shared folders can be created on the network and used for group discussions.

Another plus of working on a network is that you can stay connected to the network throughout the day. There need be no concern over connect time as there is with an Internet dial-in account. Being connected to the network constantly not only means that corporate email will be downloaded to your computer periodically, but also that any incoming Internet email will also be downloaded throughout the day.

 Using Net Folders on a Corporate Network   If you are on a corporate network, you can still take advantage of Net Folders to share information with people over the Internet. Add Internet Folders as an Outlook service by selecting Tools, Services.

MAKING YOUR INSTALLATION DECISION

While the choice of Outlook installation will mainly be dictated by how you connect to electronic mail and other shared resources (Internet Only or Corporate installation), you do have the option of using either of the configurations even if you only plan to connect to the Internet and use Internet email.

While the Internet Only configuration is best suited for Internet connected users, you may find that you want to use the Corporate installation so that you can take advantage of the faxing capabilities of Microsoft Fax (remember, WinFax is installed with the Internet Only configuration and is not quite as flexible a fax tool as Microsoft Fax). Choosing the Corporate installation for a computer connecting to the Internet via a service provider would mean that you will want to set up the Internet Only service and forgo setting up any other electronic mail services such as Exchange Server or Microsoft Mail.

Whichever installation you adopt, remember that this will give a certain look and feel to the Outlook configuration. For instance, the Internet Only configuration does not have a Services command on the Tools menu. You will also find that the Options dialog box (see Figure 3.6) will have more tabs available than the Internet Only installation because of the additional

Outlook functions provided by the Corporate installation. For more information on configuring Outlook, see Lesson 24, "Customizing Outlook."

FIGURE 3.6   The Customization options available to you in Outlook depends on the type of installation you chose when initially setting up Outlook on your computer.

Reconfiguring Your Mail Support   If you find that you've configured Outlook for one of the email configurations, such as Internet Only email, and would like to switch to the other configuration (Corporate), you can reconfigure your mail support without reinstalling Outlook. Select Tools, Options. On the Options dialog box that appears select the Mail Services tab. Then click the Reconfigure Mail Support button. The Outlook E-Mail Services screen opens. This is the same screen that appears the first time you start a new installation of Outlook (described in the "Installation Considerations" section of this lesson). Select the type of email installation you want to have and then follow the prompts to reconfigure your email setup for Outlook. You might need to place the Office 2000 or Outlook 2000 CD in your CD-ROM drive if prompted for installation files.

In this lesson you learned about the Internet Only and the Corporate email configurations for Outlook 2000. In the next lesson, you learn the various Outlook tools such as the Outlook bar.

LESSON 4

USING OUTLOOK'S TOOLS

In this lesson you learn how to change views in Outlook, as well as how to use the Outlook bar and the Folder list.

USING THE OUTLOOK BAR

Each Outlook organization tool has its own folder. You have a folder for email (Inbox), a folder for the calendar (Calendar), and so on. The Outlook bar is a tool you can use to quickly change folders in Outlook. The icons in the Outlook bar represent all of the folders available to you and provide shortcuts to getting to the contents of those folders. Figure 4.1 shows the Outlook bar.

Three shortcut groups are located within the Outlook bar: Outlook, My Shortcuts, and Other Shortcuts. Each group contains related folders in which you can work.

- **The Outlook Shortcuts Group**   This group contains folders for working with the different organizational tools in Outlook, such as the Inbox, the Calendar, Tasks, and so on.

- **The Shortcuts Group**   This group contains folders for organizing and managing your electronic mail and faxes.

- **The Other Shortcuts Group**   This group contains folders on your computer, such as My Computer, My Documents, and Favorites, which is a list of your favorite Web sites. You can use each of these folders to work with files and folders outside Outlook.

Folders within a group   Contents of selected folder

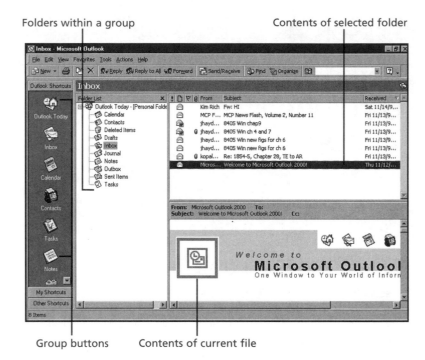

Group buttons   Contents of current file

FIGURE 4.1   Use the Outlook bar to view various items in your
work.

To switch from one group to another, click either the Outlook Shortcuts,
My Shortcuts, or Other Shortcuts button on the Outlook bar. The Outlook
group is displayed by default providing quick access to tools such as your
Inbox, Calendar, and Contacts list.

THE OUTLOOK SHORTCUTS FOLDERS

The Outlook Shortcuts group folders in the Outlook bar enable you to
access your work in Outlook. That includes your email messages,
appointments, Contacts list, and so on. Table 4.1 describes each of the
folders within the Outlook group.

TABLE 4.1   OUTLOOK GROUP FOLDERS

FOLDER	DESCRIPTION
Outlook Today	While not really a folder, the Outlook Today icon on the Outlook bar provides a summary of Calendar events, tasks, and new messages for the current day (today).
Inbox	Includes messages you've sent and received by email and fax.
Calendar	Contains your appointments, events, scheduled meetings, and so on.
Contacts	Lists names and addresses of the people with whom you communicate.
Tasks	Includes any tasks you have on your to-do list.
Journal	Contains all journal entries, such as phone logs, meeting notes, and so on.
Notes	Lists notes you write to yourself or others.
Deleted Items	Includes any items you've deleted from other folders.

THE MY SHORTCUTS GROUP FOLDERS

The My Shortcuts group folders (see Figure 4.2) provide a method of organizing your incoming and outgoing email messages. Table 4.2 describes each folder in the Mail group.

TABLE 4.2   MY SHORTCUTS FOLDERS

FOLDER	DESCRIPTION
Drafts	Contains messages that are saved but not sent
Sent Items	Stores all messages you've sent
Outbox	Contains messages to be sent
Journal	Keeps a list of your Outlook activities

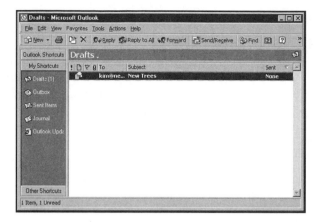

FIGURE 4.2   The My Shortcuts folder icons give you access to your email and fax messages that have been sent, are waiting to be sent, or have been saved.

 I See Other Folders in My Groups   You can add additional folders and folder icons very easily to Outlook. If you find folders other than the ones described here, they have probably been added to your particular installation of Outlook.

THE OTHER SHORTCUTS FOLDERS

The Other Shortcuts group contains folders that are on your computer but not within Outlook: My Computer, My Documents, and Favorites. You can access a document or information in any of those folders so that you can attach it to a message, add notes to it, or otherwise use it in Outlook.

For example, with My Computer, you can view the contents of both hard and floppy disks, CD-ROM drives, and so on (see Figure 4.3). Double-click a drive in the window to view its folders and files. Double-click a folder to view its contents as well. You also can attach files to messages or otherwise use the files on your hard drive with the Outlook features.

FIGURE 4.3   View your entire system through the My Computer folder in Outlook.

 Moving On Up   Use the Up One Level button on the Advanced toolbar to return to a folder or drive after you've double-clicked to expand it and view its contents.

USING THE FOLDER LIST

Outlook provides another method of viewing the folders within Outlook and your system: the Folder list. The Folder list displays the folders within any of the three groups (Outlook Shortcuts, My Shortcuts, or Other Shortcuts). From the list, you can select the folder you want to view.

To use the Folder list, first select the group (such as Outlook Shortcuts or Other Shortcuts) that contains the folders you want to view, then select a particular folder (using the appropriate shortcut) from the Outlook bar. Then click the Folder List button to display the list (see Figure 4.4).

Click here to display the Folder list

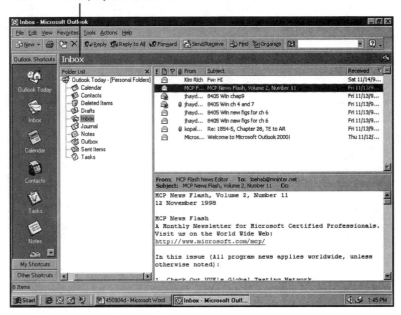

FIGURE 4.4   The Folder list shows all folders in the group you selected.

 Pinning Down the Folder List   When you click the Folder List button on a particular folder's name, the Folder list floats on top of the current folder window. Click the push pin button in the upper corner of the Folder list to "pin down" the list in the Outlook window. If you want to close the "pinned" Folder list, click its Close (X) button.

Choose any folder from the list, and the Information Viewer changes to reflect your selection. If you display another folder in the Information screen, double-click the folder to display its contents.

 A View of the Folder List   You also can open the Folder list by using the View menu.

CHANGING VIEWS

Outlook provides different views that enable you to look at the information in your various folders from a particular perspective. Each view presents the information in a different format and organizational structure.

The easiest way to select the different views provided for each of your Outlook folders is a View box that is present on the Advanced toolbar for each folder type (Inbox, Calendar, Contacts, and so on). To open the Advanced toolbar for any Outlook folder, follow these steps:

1. Point to the Standard toolbar for an Outlook folder (such as the Inbox) and right-click.

2. A shortcut menu appears, as shown in Figure 4.5. Click Advanced. The Advanced toolbar appears.

3. If you want to close the Standard toolbar after you've opened the Advanced toolbar, right-click either toolbar and then click Standard to remove the check mark. The Standard toolbar closes.

 You Only Have to Open the Advanced Toolbar Once After you've opened the Advanced toolbar for a folder, such as the Calendar or Inbox, it will be available for all the other Outlook folders.

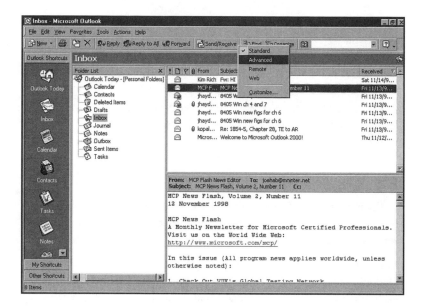

FIGURE 4.5   Right-click the Standard toolbar to open the Outlook Advanced toolbar for any folder.

Each folder—Inbox, Calendar, Contacts, and so on—has a different set of buttons on the Standard and Advanced toolbars. This is because the commands and features that you access on a toolbar will be particular to the folder that you currently have selected.

After you have the Advanced toolbar open, you can change the current view by clicking the current view drop-down box, as shown in Figure 4.6. Each current view box contains views that are appropriate for the currently selected folder on the Outlook bar.

As you can see in Figure 4.6, you can change your view of the Inbox. You can choose to see all messages (Messages), messages and their first three lines of text (Messages with AutoPreview), messages that have been tagged with a follow-up flag (By Follow Up Flag), messages from the last seven days (Last Seven Days), messages tagged with a flag for the next seven days (Flagged for Next Seven Days), messages organized by topic (By Conversation Topic), messages organized by sender (By Sender), unread messages only (Unread Messages), messages by recipient (Sent To), and messages arranged in a timeline (Message Timeline).

Current view list   Views

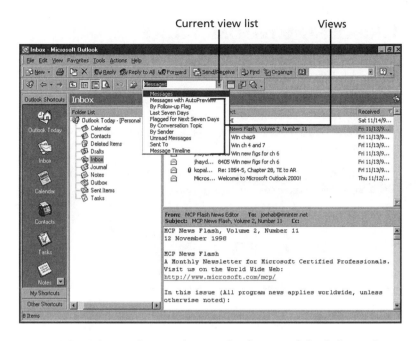

FIGURE 4.6   Select a view to change the format of the information.

Similarly, the Calendar folder—which is arranged in the
Day/Week/Month view type by default—enables you to view your
appointments and events by active appointments, by Day/Week/Month
with AutoPreview, by events, by recurring appointments, and by several
other view types.

You also can change the view type for any of your folders by selecting the
Edit menu and then pointing at Current View. The View list appears as a
submenu of Edit.

As you work your way through this book, you'll see examples of each
view type. When you change folders in Outlook, take a quick look at the
available views in the current view drop-down list.

CREATING CUSTOM VIEWS

You also can create custom views of the information in your Outlook folders. To create a custom view for one of your Outlook folders, follow these steps:

1. Click the View menu, and then point at Current View. Select Define Views. A Define Views dialog box for the currently selected folder opens.

2. Click the New button in the Define Views box. The Create a New View dialog box appears, as shown in Figure 4.7.

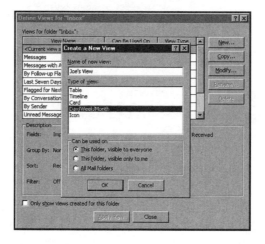

FIGURE 4.7   You can create custom views for your Outlook folders.

3. Enter a name for your new view and select a view type from the list in the Type of View box.

   The different view types that you can select for a custom view are described as follows:

   • **Table View**   Presents items in a grid of sorts—in rows and columns. Use this view type to view mail messages, tasks, and details about any item.

- **Timeline View**   Displays items as icons arranged in chronological order from left to right on a time scale. Use this to view journal entries and other items in this type of view.

- **Day/Week/Month View**   Displays items in a calendar view in blocks of time. Use this type for meetings and scheduled tasks.

- **Card View**   Presents items similar to cards in a card file. Use this to view contacts.

- **Icon View**   Provides graphic icons to represent tasks, notes, calendars, and so on.

4. After you've selected the type of view you want to create, click OK. A View Settings dialog box appears. In this box you determine which fields you want to have in the view, as well as the fonts and other view settings you want to use.

5. After you've selected the fields and view settings, click Apply View. The items in the current folder appear in the new view.

 Fields   A specific type of information that you want to appear in your custom view. For a custom Inbox view using the Timeline view type, the fields would include Received (when the message was received), Created (when the message was created), and Sent (when the message was sent).

Your new view will appear on the current view list on the Advanced toolbar. You can select it by clicking the list's drop-down arrow and then clicking the custom view's name.

Should I Design My Own Views? Designing your own views can prove complicated. Outlook provides several views for each of the folders on the Outlook bar. You may want to explore all these possibilities before you begin to create your own views.

USING OUTLOOK TODAY

A great way to get a snapshot view of your day is with Outlook Today. This feature provides a window that lists all your messages, appointments, and tasks associated with the current day.

To open the Outlook Today window, click the Go menu, then select Outlook Today. Icons for your Calendar, Messages, and Tasks appear in the Outlook Today window as shown in Figure 4.8. Items for the current day are listed below the icons.

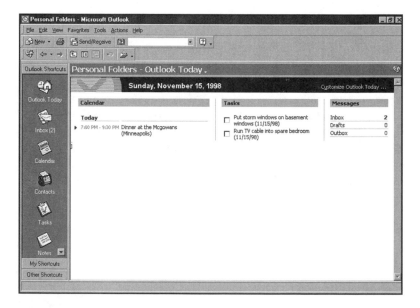

FIGURE 4.8 Outlook Today provides you with a list of all the items associated with the current day.

You can click any of the listed items (a particular appointment or task) to open the appropriate folder and view the details associated with the items. You can even update the items.

The Outlook Today window also provides a Find a Contact box that you can use to find people in your Contacts folder. Type a name in the Person text box and then click the Go button. A Contact window appears for that person. You can edit the person's information or close the Contact box by clicking the Close button.

After you have viewed the items in the Outlook Today window, you can return to any of your folders by clicking their icon on the Outlook bar. Outlook Today is an excellent way to get a handle on what your day has in store for you.

In this lesson you learned to use the Outlook bar, change and create views in Outlook, use the Folder list, and take advantage of the Outlook Today feature. In the next lesson you learn to get help in Outlook.

LESSON 5
GETTING HELP

In this lesson you learn to use the Office Assistant, to search for help on specific topics, and to use other Help features.

USING THE OFFICE ASSISTANT

You've probably noticed the Office Assistant: he's the special character who sits in the Outlook window waiting to provide you with help. You can use the Office Assistant to help you with procedures, explanations, and tasks you perform in Outlook.

To use the Office Assistant, do one of the following:

- Click the Assistant.

- Choose Help, Microsoft Outlook Help.

- Press F1.

The Assistant displays the text balloon shown in Figure 5.1 when you click it. The Office Assistant's help is context-sensitive; thus, depending on where you are in the program, the Assistant tries to offer help on related topics. If you need help on one of the suggested topics, click one of the blue option buttons.

 Context-Sensitive A help feature that senses where you are in the program—in the Inbox, using the Calendar, or creating a message, for example—and offers help on topics that are related to your current task.

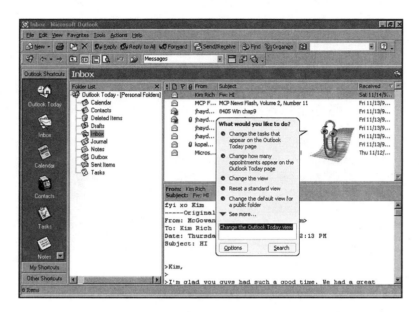

FIGURE 5.1   Use the Office Assistant to get context-sensitive help in
Outlook.

If you don't get a list of topics from the Assistant, you can enter a question in the Assistant's balloon in the search box and click Search. You
might, for example, enter "How do I print?" (or "How do I save a file?" or
any other question containing key words related to topics for which you
need help). When the Office Assistant box appears, it contains options
related to your question.

To close the Office Assistant, click the Close button or click outside the
help box.

Tricks of the Trade   When a light bulb appears over
the Assistant, this means the Assistant has help to
offer you on your current task. Click the Assistant to
see what it can offer.

You can right-click the Office Assistant and choose Hide Assistant from the shortcut menu. You can also either choose options for the Assistant or choose to use a different Assistant.

 Choosing a Different Assistant   Outlook 2000 and Microsoft Office come with several different Office Assistants. To choose a new assistant, right-click the current Assistant and select Choose Assistant from the shortcut menu. An Office Assistant Gallery box appears. Use the Next or Back buttons to choose a new Assistant, and then click OK (you may have to insert your Office CD into your CD-ROM drive to select a new Assistant).

GETTING HELP WITHOUT THE ASSISTANT

If you prefer, you can turn off the Assistant feature and access Outlook Help in a more conventional manner. Click the Assistant and on the Assistant Balloon click Options. On the Options tab deselect the check box that says Use the Office Assistant. The Assistant will be removed from the Outlook window. Now you're ready to get help from Outlook without going through the Assistant. Click the Help menu; then click Microsoft Outlook Help. The Help window appears and explains different ways to get help in Outlook.

Click the Show button on the top left of the Help window. The window expands and three tabs appear—Contents, Answer Wizard, and Index.

You will find that the Help window has the look and feel of a World Wide Web browser. When you look up a particular topic, additional information can be accessed by clicking on a highlighted item that operates as a hyperlink. This link takes you to a new set of help information. You will also find that the Help window has Back and Forward buttons that allow you to move backward and forward, respectively, through the Help information that you have viewed.

FIGURE 5.2   When you turn off the Assistant you can directly access
the Outlook Help system.

Each of the Help tabs provides you with a slightly different way to access
the help you need. The Contents tab supplies you with a list that will take
you to major groupings of information such as Outlook basics and information on specific tasks such as using the Calendar or Contacts folder.

As an example of how the Contents tab works, take a look at how it supplies you with information on working with the Calendar. Scroll down
through the alphabetical Contents listing. Each main topic is represented
by a book icon. Double-click the Using Calendar book. The Help Book
icon opens and displays a sublist of more specific topics. Double-click
Open a Calendar item in the sublist.

On the right pane of the Help window, you are provided with specific help
on how to open a Calendar item. In some cases you will find that certain
words have been highlighted in the help text. For instance in the information on opening a Calendar item, the word "item" is highlighted. Words
presented in this manner are Glossary terms. Clicking them gives you a
definition of the word.

Glossary terms Highlighted words in the Help system that provide you with a definition when you click them.

USING THE ANSWER WIZARD

Another way to get help in the Help window is to use the Answer Wizard. The Answer Wizard works exactly the same way as the Office Assistant does; you ask the Wizard questions and it supplies you with a list of topics that relate to your question. You click one of the choices provided to view help in the Help window.

To use the Answer Wizard follow these steps:

1. Click the Answer Wizard tab in the Help window. Type your question in the What would you like to do? box.

2. Click the Search button. A list of topics appears in the Select a Topic to Display box.

3. Double-click a topic and help related to the topic appears in the right pane of the Help window.

Click here for a description

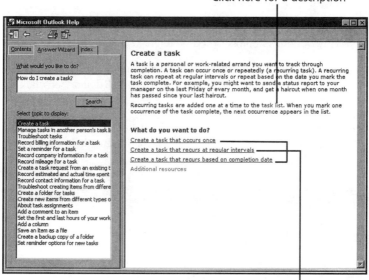

Click here for more information

FIGURE 5.3   The Answer Wizard provides you with a list of topics that you can choose from to get help with a particular feature.

USING THE INDEX

Another way to get to help from the Outlook Help window is to do keyword searches in the Help system's index. To access the Index system, click the Index tab in the Help window. The Index allows you to type in a keyword or keywords, select from a list of existing keywords, or select from a list of topics that appear based on your keywords or keywords you chose from the keyword list.

To use the Index follow these steps:

1. Type a keyword in the Type Keywords box. Notice that as you type, Outlook attempts to complete the keyword for you.

2. After typing in the keyword, click the Search button or select a more appropriate keyword from the keyword list and then click Search.

3. A list of help topics appears in the Choose a Topic box. Select the appropriate topic in the list and the associated help appears in the right pane of the Help window.

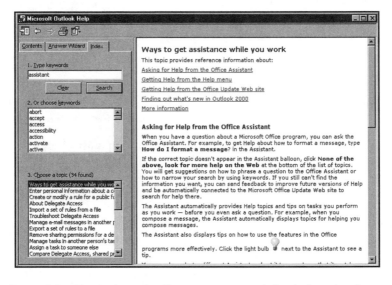

FIGURE 5.4 The Index tab allows you to search for help using keywords.

As with the other forms of help (Contents and Answer Wizard) you can use the hyperlinks provided on the Help screens to move to specific areas of the Help system. If you want to begin another keyword search, you can clear the current topics in the Choose a Topic box by clicking the Clear button.

When you've completed your search for help using the Index or have found help using the Contents or Answer Wizard tab, you can do any of the following:

- Print the topic by clicking the Print button.

- Click the Back button to view the previous Help window.

- Hide the Help tabs by clicking the Hide button.

- Click the Close (X) button to close Help.

WHAT'S THIS?

In most of its dialog boxes, Outlook includes a handy tool called a What's This button. This is the question mark button that appears at the right end of the title bar next to the Close (X) button. You can click the What's This button and then click any item in the dialog box to see an explanation or definition of the selected element. Click again to hide the help box.

More Help   Another way to use this feature is to open the Help menu and choose the What's This command. When the mouse pointer changes to a pointer with a question mark, click anything in the Outlook window that you have a question about, and a Help box explaining the item appears.

Getting Online Help for Outlook   If you find that you would like to get more help than the Outlook Help system can provide, you can look for additional help online at Microsoft's Office Web site. Click the Help menu, then select Office on the Web. Your Web browser will open and you will be taken to the Microsoft Office Update site. If you have problems connecting to the site, make sure that your modem is connected to your Internet service provider before you select the Office on the Web menu selection.

In this lesson you learned to use the Office Assistant, to search for help on specific topics, and to use other Help features. In the next lesson you learn to create electronic mail messages.

LESSON 6

CREATING MAIL

In this lesson you learn to compose a message, format text, check your spelling, and send mail. You also learn to use different email formats such as text-only and HTML mail.

COMPOSING A MESSAGE

You can send a message to anyone for whom you have an address, whether his or her address is in your address book, your list of contacts, or scribbled on a Post-It note. In addition to sending a message to one or more recipients, you can send copies of a message to other people you have an email address for or those whom are listed on your various address lists

 Compose Your Messages Offline If you connect to an Internet service provider and don't want to waste precious connect time while you compose email messages, you can create new messages in Outlook without being connected to the Internet. New messages that you send will be placed in your Outbox until you connect to the Internet and actually send them to their final destination.

ENTERING AN ADDRESS IN A MESSAGE

You can either use the address book to choose the names of recipients to whom you want to send new messges or have the email address automatically placed in the To: box when you forward messages or send a reply. Using the address book also makes sending carbon copies and blind carbon copies easy.

 Blind Carbon Copy   A blind carbon copy (Bcc) of a message is a copy that's sent to someone in secret; the other recipients have no way of knowing that you're sending the message to someone as a blind carbon copy.

To address a message, follow these steps:

1. Choose Compose, New Mail Message from the Outlook Inbox window, or click the New Message button on the toolbar. A new message window appears (see Figure 6.1).

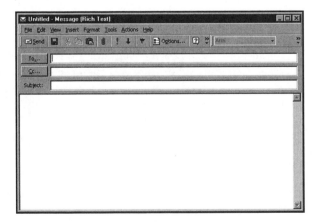

FIGURE 6.1   Compose a new message in the Untitled - Message window.

2. In the Message window, click the To button to display the Select Names dialog box. If you have not added any names to your Address book or Contacts list, no names will be available; read the following tip to learn how to add an address or simply type the email address in the To text box. If you choose to type the email address directly in the To text box, you can then skip steps 3 through 7 (for more information on adding people to your Address book or Contacts list, see Lessons 12 and 13).

Adding People to Your Address or Contacts List If your Contacts or Address list is currently empty, you can still quickly add a new address to either list and then use it for the To address on the current new message. When the Select Names dialog box appears, select the list you want to add the new name to from the Show Names drop-down box at the top of the dialog box. Then click the New button. Enter the recipient's name in the Display Name box and then enter his or her email address in the Email Address box. Then click OK. The person's Display Name will be placed in the message's To box, addressing the message for you.

3. Click the address book drop-down list box at the top right of the dialog box and choose the Postoffice Address List, Contacts List, Global Address List, or the Personal Address Book as appropriate. This allows you to view to names in a particular address book.

4. From the list of addresses that appears on the left, choose the name of the intended recipient and select the To button. Outlook copies the name to the Message Recipients list. (You can add multiple names if you want.)

5. (Optional) Select the names of anyone to whom you want to send a carbon copy, and click the Cc button to transfer those names to the Message Recipients list.

6. (Optional) Select the names of anyone to whom you want to send a blind carbon copy and click the Bcc button. Figure 6.2 shows a distribution group listing as the To recipient of a message.

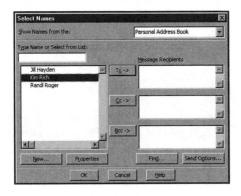

FIGURE 6.2   Address messages quickly with the Select Names dialog box.

7. Click OK to return to the Message window.

You can also easily send email to any people whose addresses you keep in your Contacts folder. How to use and maintain the Contacts folder is covered in Lesson 12, "Using the Contact and Personal Address Books."

8. Click in the text area, and then enter the text of the message. You do not have to press the Enter key at the end of a line; Outlook automatically wraps the text at the end of a line for you. You can use the Delete and Backspace keys to edit the text you enter.

9. When you finish typing the message, you can send the message to your Outbox (see "Sending Mail" later in this lesson), or you can check the spelling and formatting as described in the following sections.

No Address!   If you try to send a message without entering an address, Outlook (or the Office Assistant) displays a message that there must be at least one name in the To box. Either type in an entry or insert an entry from your Address Book or Outlook Contacts list.

FORMATTING TEXT

You can change the format of the text in your message to make it more attractive, to make it easier to read, or to add emphasis. Any formatting you do transfers to the recipient with the message if the recipient has Outlook or another email client that can work with Outlook Rich Text (formerly known as Microsoft Exchange Rich Text) or HTML messages. However, if the recipient doesn't have an email package that can handle these special message formats, formatting may not transfer. Many Internet email clients do not offer this capability. Most corporate email clients, such as Lotus Notes and Novell GroupWise, do allow the sending and receiving of messages in Rich Text Format. You should keep in mind that if you send a Rich Text or HTML message to a person who has an email client that cannot handle special formatting, they will receive the message in plain text.

Outlook Rich Text (Exchange Rich Text)   A special email format developed by Microsoft for use with Microsoft mail systems. Outlook 2000 can send and receive messages in the Exchange Rich Text format. This allows you to send and receive messages with special formatting such as bold, italic, fonts, and other special characters and graphics.

HTML   Hypertext Markup Language is used to design Web pages for the World Wide Web. Outlook 2000 can send messages in this format, providing you with a number of formatting options.

You format text in two ways. You can format the text after you type it by selecting it and then choosing a font, size, or other attribute; or you can select the font, size, or other attribute and then enter the text.

To format the text in your message, follow these steps:

1. If the Formatting toolbar is not showing, choose View, Toolbars, Formatting. Figure 6.3 shows a message with the Formatting toolbar displayed. Table 6.1 explains the buttons on this toolbar.

 Formatting Toolbar Buttons Unavailable! If you've selected to send your messages as text-only, the Formatting toolbar buttons will be unavailable to you. Only messages sent in Microsoft Exchange Rich Text format or HTML format can be formatted. See the section in this lesson on "Sending HTML Messages" for more information. If you have installed Outlook for Internet email only, you will also find that when you select the Format command, only Plain Text and Rich Text (HTML) are available as choices.

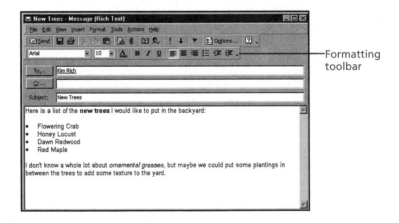

FIGURE 6.3   Use the Formatting toolbar to modify your message text.

TABLE 6.1   FORMATTING TOOLBAR BUTTONS

BUTTON	NAME
Heading 1	Style (only when using HTML Format)
Times New Roman	Font
24	Font Size
A	Font Color
B	Bold
I	Italic
U	Underline
	Align Left
	Center
	Align Right
	Bullets
	Numbering
	Decrease Indent
	Increase Indent

My Toolbars Look Completely Different!   If you've selected to use Microsoft Word as your email editor, the toolbars that are present in the new message window will reflect those that you have selected in your Word installation. You will find that many of the toolbar icons used on the Word toolbar are also found on the Outlook toolbars. Table 6.1 should provide you with the necessary cross-references to format your email message text as outlined in this lesson.

2. To apply a font to the selected or about-to-be-entered text, click the down arrow in the Font box on the Formatting toolbar. Scroll through the font list, if necessary, to view all fonts on the system, and click the font you want to apply to the text. You can also apply a style to selected text in the message. Click the Style drop-down arrow on the Formatting toolbar. The styles available range from a set of predefined heading styles to special styles such as Directory List and Menu List.

Quick Format   You can also format text by choosing Format, Font and selecting a font, size, style, and so on from the Font dialog box. You also can assign bullets and alignment to text by choosing Format, Paragraph.

3. Assign a size by clicking the down arrow beside the Font Size drop-down list and choosing the size; alternatively, you can enter a size in the Font Size text box.

4. To choose a color, click the Color button and select a color from the palette box that appears.

5. Choose a type style to apply to text by clicking the Bold, Italic, or Underline buttons on the Formatting toolbar.

6. Choose an alignment by selecting the Align Left, Center, or Align Right button from the Formatting toolbar.

7. Add bullets to a list by clicking the Bullet button on the Formatting toolbar. If you prefer a numbered list, click the Numbering button.

8. Create text indents or remove indents in half-inch increments by clicking the Increase Indent or Decrease Indent buttons. (Each time you click the Indent button, the indent changes by half an inch.)

 Using Undo If you assign formatting to your text and don't particularly like it, click Edit, Undo to remove the last formatting that you did.

SENDING HTML MESSAGES

Another alternative for sending messages with formatted text is the HTML format. HTML stands for Hypertext Markup Language and is the language used to design Web pages for the World Wide Web. You can choose to send your email messages in this format by following these steps:

1. Click Tools, Options. The Options dialog box appears.

2. Click the Mail Format tab (see Figure 6.4).

 Include Hyperlinks If you send HTML or Rich Text Format messages, you can include hyperlinks. Hyperlinks are Web addresses and email addresses that can be accessed by clicking them in the message. Just type the Web address or email address, and the hyperlink will be created automatically.

3. To select the message format, click the Send in This Message Format drop down box. Select HTML, Outlook Rich Text, or Plain Text. If you want to use Microsoft Word as your email editor, click the Use Microsoft Word to Edit Email Messages check box.

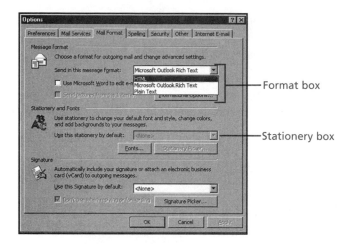

FIGURE 6.4   You can select to send your messages in HTML, Outlook Rich Text, or Plain Text Formats.

4. Click OK to close the dialog box.

If you choose to use the HTML format in the Options box, you can also select special stationery to send your messages on. Click the Use This Stationery by Default drop-down box. Outlook provides a number of HTML stationery types. To see a preview of the stationery types listed, click the Stationery Picker button.

Using the HTML format for your messages provides you with the greatest number of possibilities as far as formatting and graphics in email messages. Remember, however, that you can only take advantage of the HTML format if the receiver of your message is using Outlook or another email client that can read a message in HTML.

HTML Formatting with No Coding   When you select the HTML format for your email messages, this doesn't mean that you will have to actually write HTML code to format the various elements in the message. All you have to do is select heading and other styles (that will use HTML formatting automatically) by clicking Format and then Style.

SENDING TEXT-ONLY MESSAGES

If you send most of your messages to recipients who do not use Outlook 2000 or another email client that can take advantage of Rich Text or HTML-formatted messages, you may want to set your default message type to text only. This sends all your messages in plain text that can be read by all email clients.

To select Plain Text as your message format, follow these steps:

1. Click Tools, Options. The Options dialog box appears.

2. Click the Mail Format tab.

3. Click the Send in This Message Format drop-down box, and select Plain Text.

4. Click OK to close the dialog box.

CHECKING SPELLING

To make a good impression and to maintain your professional image, you should check the spelling in your mail messages before you send them. Outlook includes a spelling checker you can use for that purpose. You'll notice your grammar is automatically checked, as well.

To check the spelling in a message, follow these steps:

1. In the open message, choose Tools, Spelling and Grammar, or press F7. If the spelling checker finds a word whose spelling it questions, it displays the Spelling dialog box (shown in Figure 6.5). If no words are misspelled, a dialog box appears saying the spelling and grammar check is complete; choose OK to close the dialog box.

2. You can do any of the following in response to the word Outlook questions in the Spelling dialog box:

   Not in Dictionary   Enter the correct spelling in this text box.

   Suggestions   Select the correct spelling in this text box, and it automatically appears in the Change To text box.

Ignore   Click this button to continue the spelling check without changing this occurrence of the selected word.

Ignore All   Click this button to continue the spelling check without changing any occurrence of the word in question throughout this message.

Change   Click this button to change this particular occurrence of the word in question to the spelling in the Change To text box.

Change All   Click this button to change the word in question to the spelling listed in the Change To text box every time the spelling checker finds the word in this message.

Add   Click this button to add the current spelling of the word in question to the dictionary so that Outlook will not question future occurrences of this spelling.

Undo   Click this button to reverse the last spelling change you made, thus returning the word to its original spelling.

Cancel   Click this button to quit the spelling check.

FIGURE 6.5   Check your spelling before sending a message.

3. When the spelling check is complete, Outlook displays a message box telling you it's done. Click OK to close the dialog box.

Set Your Spelling Options   Click the Options button in the Spelling dialog box to set options that tell Outlook to do such things as ignore words with numbers, ignore original message text in forwarded messages or replies, always check spelling before sending, and so on.

SENDING MAIL

When you're ready to send your mail message, do one of the following:

- Click the Send button.
- Choose File, Send.
- Press Ctrl+Enter.

Signature   You can automatically add a signature file (this can include text and images) to your email messages. Choose Tools, Options to open the Options dialog box and then select the Mail Format tab. Click the Signature Picker button at the bottom of the dialog box. The Signature Picker dialog box will open. Click the New button and follow the steps provided on the Create New signature screens. Once you've created a signature or signatures, you can quickly add it to any message by choosing Insert, Signature; all the signatures that you have created will appear on the menu. Select the signature from the list that you want to use in the message that you are currently composing.

Using Windows NT 4.0?   You'll need to check your rights and permissions in relation to sending email within your network. Ask your system administrator for more information.

RECALLING A MESSAGE

If you configured Outlook for Corporate email, you can recall messages that you send over your corporate network and over the Internet. You can only recall messages that have not been opened or moved to another folder. If you want to recall a message on your corporate network, the individual from whom you are recalling the message must be logged on.

To recall a sent message, follow these steps:

1. Click the My Shorcuts button on the Outlook bar and then select the Sent Items Folder.

2. Double-click to open the message that you want to recall.

3. In the Message window, click the Tools menu, then click Recall This Message. The Recall This Message dialog box will open.

4. To recall the message click the Delete Unread Copies of This Message option button, then click OK. A notice appears in the Message window (upper-left corner) letting you know that you are attempting to recall this message.

5. Click File, Save to save the message with the recall option. Close the message.

6. You will eventually receive a notification in your Inbox (as new mail) notifying you whether the recall was successful.

In this lesson, you learned to compose a message, format text, check your spelling, and send mail. You also learned how to select different email formats such as HTML and Plain Text. You also learned how to recall a message. In the next lesson, you learn to work with received mail.

LESSON 7
WORKING WITH RECEIVED MAIL

In this lesson you learn to read your mail, save an attachment, answer mail, and close a message.

READING MAIL

When you log on to Outlook, your Inbox folder appears, and any new messages you've received are downloaded from your company's mail server. If you use Internet Mail, you will have to connect to your Internet Service Provider to download your mail using Outlook. Then any new mail will be placed in your Inbox (see Figure 7.1). If you watch closely, when you connect to your network or Internet Service Provider a down-loading mail icon appears in the lower right of the Outlook window, showing you that new mail is being received.

 My Outlook Doesn't Open to the Inbox If Outlook opens to Outlook Today, click the Inbox folder on the Outlook bar or click the Messages link in Outlook Today. Either of these alternatives will take you to your Inbox. You can also make sure that Outlook opens to your Inbox by changing the Advanced options found in the Options dialog box. Customizing settings like this are discussed in Chapter 24, "Customizing Outlook."

As you can see in Figure 7.1, the Inbox provides important information about each message. For example, one message has been labeled as high priority, one is low priority, and one message has an attachment. Messages that have already been replied to are marked with a curved reply arrow. You'll learn about priorities and attachments in Lesson 11, "Setting Mail Options." In addition, the status bar at the bottom of the Inbox window indicates how many items the Inbox folder contains and how many of those items are unread.

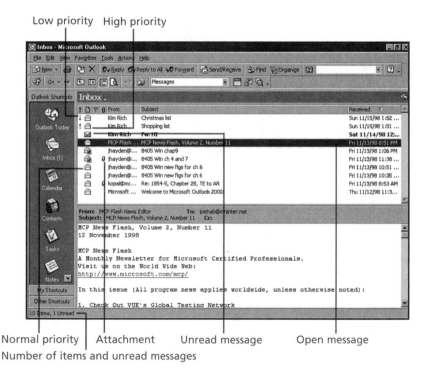

Low priority · High priority

Normal priority | Attachment   Unread message   Open message
Number of items and unread messages

FIGURE 7.1 The Inbox provides information related to your received messages: the sender, subject, date received, and priority and attachment icons.

Welcome! The first time you log on, you may find an Outlook welcome message from Microsoft in your Inbox. After you read the message, you can delete it by selecting it and pressing the Delete key.

To read a message, you can click it, and its contents will appear in the Outlook Preview Pane. You can also open a message in its own window; double-click a mail message to open it. Figure 7.2 shows an open message.

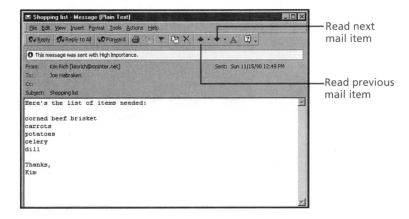

Read next mail item

Read previous mail item

FIGURE 7.2   The Message window displays the message and some tools for handling this message or moving on to another.

To read the next or previous mail message in the Inbox, click the Previous Item or the Next Item button on the toolbar. Or you can open the View menu, choose Previous or Next, and choose Item.

 Item   Outlook uses the word *item* to describe a mail message, an attached file, an appointment or meeting, a task, and so on. Item is a generic term in Outlook that describes the currently selected element.

You can mark messages as read or unread by choosing Edit, Mark as Read, or Mark as Unread. Outlook automatically marks messages as read when you open them. But you might want to mark messages yourself once in a while (as a reminder, for example). Additionally, you can mark all of the messages in the Inbox as read at one time by choosing Edit, Mark All as Read. You might want to mark mail messages as read so you don't read them again; you might want to mark important mail as unread so you'll be sure to open it and read it again.

No Mail? If you don't see any new mail in your Inbox, click the Send and Receive button on the tool-bar, or choose Tools, Check for New Mail, and Outlook will update your mail for you. Choose Tools, Check for New Mail On to specify a service other than the default. See Lesson 24, "Customizing Outlook," for more information.

SAVING AN ATTACHMENT

You will often receive messages that have files or other items attached. In the Inbox list of messages, an attachment is represented by a paper clip icon beside the message. You'll want to save any attachments sent to you so you can open, modify, print, or otherwise use the document. Messages can contain multiple attachments.

 What About Viruses? There is a (slight) chance that an attachment to a message can be infected with a virus. Computer viruses can really wreak havoc on your computer system. When you receive an email message from someone you don't know and that mes-sage has an attachment, the best thing to do is delete the message without opening it or the attachment. In cases where you save an attachment to your com-puter, you may want to check the file with an antivirus program before you actually open the file.

To save an attachment, follow these steps:

1. Open the message containing an attachment by double-clicking the message. The attachment appears as an icon in the message text (see Figure 7.3).

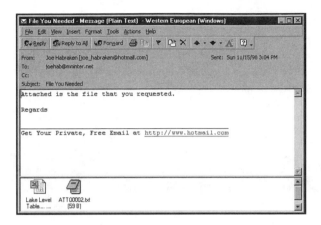

FIGURE **7.3**   An icon represents the attached file.

2. (Optional) You can open the attachment from within the message by double-clicking the icon. The application in which the document was created—Word or Excel, for example—opens and displays the document in the window, ready for you to read. Close the application by choosing File, Exit.

3. In the message, select the attachment you want to save and choose File, Save Attachments. The Save Attachments dialog box appears (see Figure 7.4).

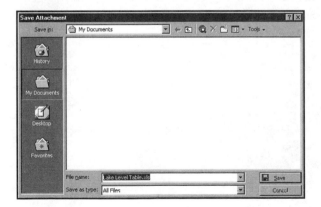

FIGURE **7.4**   Save the attachment to a convenient folder.

4. Choose the folder in which you want to save the attachment, and click Save. You can change the name of the file, if you want. You can open the attachment at any time from the application in which it was created. The dialog box closes and returns to the Message window.

Use the Right Mouse Button   You can also quickly save an attachment by right-clicking the attachment icon. On the shortcut menu that appears, click Save As and then save the attachment to an appropriate folder.

ANSWERING MAIL

You might want to reply to a message after you read it. The Message window enables you to answer a message immediately, or at a later time if you prefer. To reply to any given message, follow these steps:

1. Select the message in the Inbox window and then click the Reply button on the Inbox toolbar.

   If you have the message open, you can click the Reply button in the message window or choose Compose, Reply. The Reply Message window appears, with the original message in the message text area and the sender of the message already filled in for you (see Figure 7.5).

Reply to All   If you receive a message that has also been sent to others—as either a message or a carbon copy (Cc)—you can click the Reply to All button to send your reply to each person who received the message.

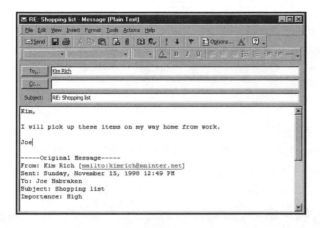

FIGURE 7.5   You can reply to a message quickly and easily.

2. The insertion point is in the message text area, ready for you to enter your reply. Enter the text.

3. When you finish your reply, click the Send button or choose File, Send. Outlook sends the message.

If you are using Outlook as your Internet mail program, clicking the Send button only places the reply message in your Outlook Outbox. You must click the Send and Receive button on the Outlook toolbar to empty the Outbox and send your messages on to their respective recipients. You can also configure Outlook to send messages immediately. See Lesson 24 for information on customizing Outlook.

 Reminder   The next time you open a message to which you've replied, you'll see a reminder at the top of the Message tab that tells you the date and time you sent your reply. And don't forget that the purple arrow next to a message in the Inbox window shows that the message has been replied to.

PRINTING MAIL

You can print mail messages whether they're open or not. To print an unopened message, select the message in the message list of the Inbox or other folder and choose File, Print. If the message is already open, you can follow these steps:

1. Open the message in Outlook.

2. Use one of the following methods to tell Outlook to print:

   - Click the Print button on the toolbar to print using defaults.

   - Choose the File, Print command to view the Print dialog box.

   - Press Ctrl+P.

3. In the Print dialog box, click OK to print one copy of the entire message using the printer's default settings.

> **More Print Info**   See Lesson 19, "Printing in Outlook," for detailed information about configuring pages, setting up the printer, and so on.

CLOSING A MESSAGE

When you finish a message, you can close it in any of the following ways:

   - Choose File, Close.

   - Click the Control-menu button and click Close.

   - Press Alt+F4.

   - Click the Close (X) button in the title bar of the Message window.

In this lesson, you learned to read your mail, save an attachment, answer mail, and close a message. In the next lesson, you learn to manage your mail messages.

LESSON 8

MANAGING ELECTRONIC MAIL

In this lesson you learn to delete and undelete messages, forward messages, and organize messages by saving them to folders. You also work with the Outlook Rules Wizard and the Organize tool, which provide a way to automate certain mail management tasks.

DELETING MAIL

You will find that you may want to store certain important messages, but, for the most part, you'll definitely want to read much of the mail that you receive and then delete it. After you've answered a question or responded to a request, you probably won't need a reminder of that transaction. You can easily delete messages in Outlook when you're finished with them.

To delete a mail message that is open, do one of the following:

- Choose File, Delete.

- Press Ctrl+D.

- Click the Delete button on the toolbar.

If you have modified the message in any way, a confirmation message appears from the Office Assistant or as a message dialog box. Otherwise, the message is deleted without warning.

If you're in the Inbox and you want to delete one or more messages from the message list, select the single message to delete (or hold down the Ctrl key and click each message). Then do one of the following:

- Press the Delete key.

- Click the Delete button on the toolbar.

UNDELETING ITEMS

If you change your mind and want to get back items you've deleted, you can usually retrieve them from the Deleted Items folder. By default, when you delete an item, it doesn't disappear from your system; it merely moves to the Deleted Items folder. Items stay in the Deleted Items folder until you delete them from that folder—at which point they are unrecoverable. To retrieve a deleted item from the Deleted Items folder click the Undo Delete icon in the Advanced toolbar. Or if multiple messages have to be undeleted, follow these steps:

1. Click the scroll down arrow on the Outlook bar to locate the Deleted Items folder.

2. Click the Deleted Items icon in the Outlook bar to open the folder.

3. Select the items you want to retrieve, and drag them to the folder containing the same type of items on the Outlook bar. Alternatively, you can choose Edit, Move to Folder and choose the folder to which you want to move the selected items.

EMPTYING THE DELETED ITEMS FOLDER

If you're really sure you want to delete the items in the Deleted Items folder, you can erase them from your system. To delete items in the Deleted Items folder, follow these steps:

1. In the Outlook bar, choose the Outlook Shortcuts or My Shortcuts group and then select the Deleted Items folder. All deleted items in that folder appear in the message list, as shown in Figure 8.1.

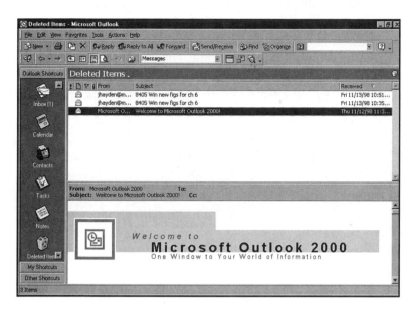

FIGURE 8.1   Deleted messages remain in the Deleted Items folder until you permanently delete them.

2. To permanently delete an item, select it in the Deleted Items folder and click the Delete button or choose Edit, Delete.

3. Outlook displays a confirmation dialog box asking if you're sure you want to permanently delete the message. Choose Yes to delete the selected item. You also can choose more than one item at a time by holding down the Shift or Ctrl key as you click each item.

4. To switch back to the Inbox or another folder, select the folder from either the Outlook bar or the Folders list.

Automatic Permanent Delete   You can set Outlook to permanently delete the contents of the Deleted Items folder every time you exit the program. To do so, choose Tools, Options, and click the Other tab. In the General Settings area, select Empty the Deleted Items Folder Upon Exiting and click OK.

FORWARDING MAIL

Suppose you want to forward mail you receive from a coworker to another person who has an interest in the message. You can forward any message you receive, and you can even add comments to the message if you want.

 Forward Mail When you forward mail, you send a message you received to another person on the network; you can add your own comments to the forwarded mail, if you want.

You forward an open message or a message selected in the message list in the Inbox in the same way. To forward mail, follow these steps:

 1. Select or open the message you want to forward. Then click the Forward button or choose Actions, Forward. The FW Message window appears (see Figure 8.2).

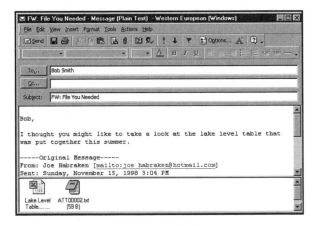

FIGURE 8.2 When you forward a message, the original message appears at the bottom of the message window.

2. In the To text box, enter the names of the people to whom you want to forward the mail. (If you want to choose a person's name from a list, click the To button to display the Select Names dialog box, and then select the person's name.) Lesson 12, "Using the Contacts and Personal Address Books," explains more about using the Address Book. If you enter multiple names in the To box, separate the names with a semicolon and a space.

3. (Optional) In the Cc text box, enter the names of anyone to whom you want to forward *copies* of the message (or click the Cc... button and choose the name from the list that appears).

4. In the message area of the window, enter any message you want to send with the forwarded text. The text you type will be a different color.

 Attachments If the message that you forward contains attached files, the attachments will also be forwarded.

5. Click the Send button or choose File, Send.

SAVING MAIL TO A FOLDER

Although you'll delete some mail after you read and respond to it, you'll want to save other messages for future reference. You can save a message to any folder you want, but you should use a logical filing system to ensure that you can find each message again later. Outlook offers several methods for organizing your mail.

The easiest method of saving mail to a folder is to move it to one of Outlook's built-in Mail folders (as described in Lesson 4, "Using Outlook's Tools"). You can use any of the folders to store your mail, or you can create new folders. Lesson 10, "Organizing Messages," describes how to create your own folders within Outlook.

To move messages to an existing folder, follow these steps:

1. Select one message (by clicking it) or select multiple messages (by Ctrl+clicking). You can select an entire series of messages by clicking the first message and then Shift+clicking the last.

 Making Backup Copies You can also copy a message to another folder as a backup. To do so, choose Edit, Copy to Folder.

2. Choose Edit, Move to Folder or click the Move to Folder button on the toolbar and then click Move to Folder. The Move Items dialog box appears (see Figure 8.3).

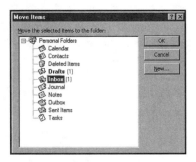

FIGURE 8.3 Choose the folder to which you want to move the selected message(s).

3. Select the folder you want to move the item to and click OK. Outlook moves the item to the folder for you.

 Quickly Creating Contacts or Tasks from Email When you select the Move to Folder button on the toolbar, you are provided with choices for Contacts and Tasks on the drop-down menu. Select either of these choices to quickly create a new contact or task from the selected email message or messages. For more information on creating contacts or tasks from messages see Lesson 21, "Integrating Items."

To view the message(s) you've moved, choose the folder from the
Outlook bar or the Folders list. Then click the item you want to view.

Attachments Move with Messages   When you move
messages to a folder other than the Inbox, any attachments to the message move to the new folder with
the message. Attachments are really part of a message
just as the text of the message is.

USING THE ORGANIZE TOOL

Outlook 98 provides an easy-to-use tool that can help you move, delete,
or color-code received and sent mail, called the Organize tool. The
Organize tool can even help you deal with annoying junk email that you
receive. The Organize feature centers on the email address of the sender
of the particular message you select and uses it to find all the messages in
the Inbox sent by this person.

The Organize tool provides you with two different possibilities: the Move
message command and the Create a Rule command. Each of these
avenues for moving messages to a particular Outlook folder have their
own area and set of command buttons in the Organize pane.

If you want to manually move the selected message to a new location,
you can use Move message. However, if you receive additional messages
from this individual at a later time, you will have to again manually move
the messages to the new location.

To manage future messages from an individual, use the Create a Rule
command. This creates a rule that will automatically move new messages
from the individual to the new location. That way, you can find all the
messages from a particular person in the same place when you need them
(both the messages you move manually and the messages moved by the
rule will end up in the same folder).

Rules   A set of conditions (such as a particular email
address, or message content) that you identify to
move, delete, or manage incoming email messages.

Rules and Attachments The rules that you create to organize your messages can look at the sender, receiver, message subject, and message text. Attachments to a message are not governed by the rules that you create, and so the content of file attachments to a message do not govern how they are handled by the Organize tool or rules that you create.

To use the Organize tool to manage messages from a particular sender, follow these steps:

1. Select a message from the person in your Inbox.

2. Click the Tools menu, and then click Organize; or click the Organize button on the toolbar. The Organize window appears (see Figure 8.4).

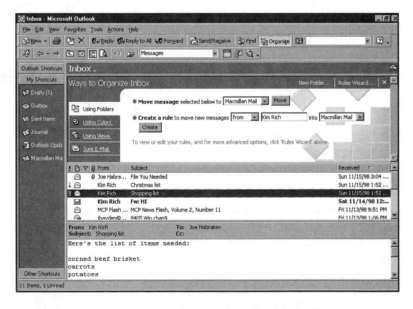

FIGURE 8.4 The Organize tool can help you manage messages using folders, colors, and views.

The Organize tool helps you manage and organize your messages using these methods:

- **Folders**   This method is used to move or delete messages.

- **Colors**   Color-codes the messages according to the rule you create.

- **Views**   Uses the rule to categorize messages by their view (Flagged, By Sender, and so on).

A special category is also provided for dealing with junk email.

To manually move the currently selected message in your Inbox, follow these steps:

1. Click Using Folders. The email address of the person who sent you the selected email will appear in the From box.

2. In the Move Message Selected Below To box, click the drop-down arrow and select the Outlook folder you would like to move the message to.

3. Click the Move button and the message will be moved to the new location.

4. If you want to move other messages, select the message in the message pane and then repeat steps 2 and 3.

As already mentioned, you can manage any new messages you receive from a particular individual by creating a rule that automatically moves these new messages to a folder of your choice. To create a new rule for the sender of the currently selected message in your Inbox, follow these steps:

1. Click Using Folders. The email address of the person who sent you the selected email will appear in the From box.

2. In the Create a Rule to Move New Messages drop-down box, make sure From is selected.

3. In the Into box, click the drop-down arrow and select the name of the folder you want to move the messages to. If you want to move the message to a folder that is not listed on the drop-down list, click Other Folder.

4. When you have selected the folder that the messages will be placed in by the rule, click Create.

You will get a short message in the Organize window that says Done. Now new messages from the individual will be moved to the new location because of the rule that you created.

The Organize tool also provides you with an automatic strategy for dealing with annoying junk mail. Click Junk E-mail in the Organize window. The Organize tool allows you to either color code junk mail and adult content email or to move these kinds of email to a folder of your choice. In most situations, junk email and other unwanted email can be moved directly to the Deleted Items folder, which can then be easily discarded. Outlook automatically identifies these types of mail messages as you receive them by using a list of keywords as identifiers.

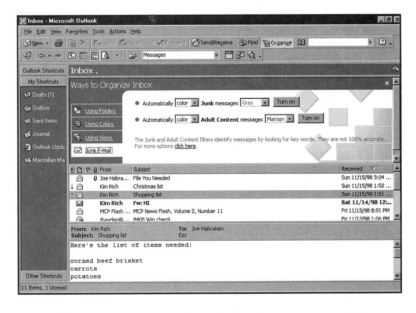

FIGURE 8.5 The Organize tool's Junk E-mail manager can help you deal with incoming junk mail.

To color code Junk messages or Adult Content messages make sure the Automatically drop-down box for each junk mail type contains the choice color. Then use the appropriate color drop-down box to select the color you want to use to code these messages as they are received. After you have selected the color, click the Turn On button to begin color coding all new messages that are identified as Junk mail or Adult Content mail by Outlook.

To send Junk messages or Adult Content messages directly to a specific folder, select Move in the Automatically drop-down box for either type of message. In the Messages To drop-down box for either message type select Junk Mail or Deleted Items to send mail messages directly to either of these folders. You can also send these messages directly to an alternative folder of your choice by clicking Other Folder. Once you have selected the folder you want to send these messages to, click the Turn On button. Messages identified as Junk mail or Adult Content mail by Outlook will be sent directly to the folder you specified.

You can also click the For More Options Click Here selection at the bottom of the Organize pane to access additional options related to Junk mail and Adult Content. Links are provided so that you can access the list of email addresses that you have identified as sources of Junk mail or Adult Content. Any email address on these lists is use to identify incoming email that should be color coded or moved to a specific folder by the Organize tool. After you have completed your selections in the Organize window, click its Close button.

You can quickly add email addresses to the Junk mail or Adult Content list by right-clicking on any message in your Inbox. A shortcut menu will appear; point at Junk E-mail on the menu, and then select either Add to Junk Senders List or Add to Adult Content Senders List from the cascading menu that opens. This will add this email to the list marking it as a source of junk mail or adult content messages.

USING THE RULES WIZARD

If the Organize tool isn't able to manage your email to the degree that you desire, you can create more advanced rules for managing messages using the Outlook Rules Wizard. The Wizard allows you to create rules using simple sentences that can do some pretty sophisticated things.

To open the Rules Wizard, follow these steps:

1. Click Tools, Rules Wizard. The Rules Wizard dialog box appears (see Figure 8.6).

   All the rules previously created using the Organize tool will appear in the Rules Description box. You can copy, modify, rename, or delete a rule in this dialog box. You can also change a rule's priority by selecting a rule and then moving it up or down using the Move Up or Move Down buttons.

FIGURE 8.6 The Rules Wizard helps you create rules for managing mail messages.

2. To create a new rule, click the New button. The Rules Wizard walks you through the rule creation process. The first screen asks you to select the type of rule you want to create, such as Check Messages When They Arrive, or Notify Me When Important Messages Arrive (see Figure 8.7)

3. Select the type of rule you want to create, and then click Next.

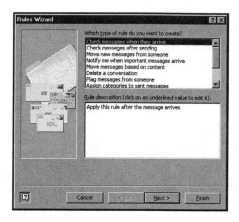

FIGURE 8.7 In the Rules Wizard, you select the type of rule you want to create.

4. The next screen asks you to select conditions that will be used by the new rule. These conditions range from messages sent directly to you, to where your name appears in the message address (To, CC, etc.), to specific words in the body of the message, to email addresses that you have placed on your Junk email list. Use the check boxes provided to select the condition or conditions for your new rule. Click Next to continue.

 Conditions That Require Input from You   Some conditions such as "with specific words in the body," or "from people or distribution list" require that you provide a list of words or people for the condition to use. Conditions requiring additional information have an underlined selection for you to click.

5. The next screen asks you to decide what the rule should do to a message that meets the rules criteria. Several choices are provided, such as move it to the specified folder, or delete it (see Figure 8.8). Make your selections in the check boxes provided. Then click Next to continue.

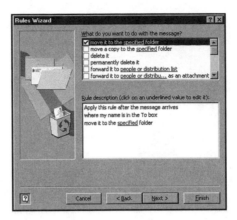

FIGURE 8.8   You determine the type of action you want Outlook to take when it finds a message that meets the rule's criteria.

6. The next screen provides you with the opportunity to add any exceptions to the rule. These exceptions can include "except if sent only to me" or "except where my name is not in the To or Cc box." You add them by clicking the check box next to a particular exception. You can select multiple exceptions or choose to have no exceptions to the rules. Then click Next to continue.

7. The Rules Wizard's final screen asks you to type a name for your new rule. After you've done that, click Finish. The new rule will appear in the Rules Wizard dialog box. You can create more new rules or click OK to close the dialog box.

When you use the Rules Wizard for the first time, you may want to create a simple rule or two that handle messages that you do not consider extremely important. A poorly designed rule could delete important messages that you receive. A good rule of thumb is to use the Organize tool first and let it create simple rules, and if you need more advanced message management help, use the Rules Wizard.

In this lesson, you learned to forward messages, delete messages, and organize messages by saving them to folders. You also learned how to use the Organize tool and the Rules Wizard to help you manage your email messages. In the next lesson, you learn to work with address books.

LESSON 9

ATTACHING ITEMS TO A MESSAGE

In this lesson you learn to attach a file and Outlook items to a message. You also learn how to insert an object in the other Outlook items, such as the calendar.

ATTACHING A FILE

You can attach any type of file to an Outlook message, which makes for a convenient way of sending your files over the network to your coworkers or send ng family pictures (that have been scanned) or other files to people using your Internet email. You might send Word documents, Excel spreadsheets, a PowerPoint presentation, or any other document you create with your Windows 98/NT applications. If you can get the file on your computer you can attach it to an email message.

 HTML Becomes Text If you send a message to someone who uses an email client that cannot read HTML messages, the message will appear as text. You must attach any pictures or other items to the message as an attachment if you want the user on the receiving end to view them.

When you send an attached file, it appears as an icon in a special attachment pane at the bottom of the message window. When the recipient gets the file, he or she can open it by double-clicking or save it for later use.

However, the recipient must have the source program that you used to create the file on his or her computer. For instance, if you send a colleague a Microsoft Word file, he must have Microsoft Word in order to view the file he receives. Microsoft also supplies viewers for Microsoft Word and PowerPoint documents. These programs can be used to view Word and PowerPoint documents without having the full-blown software installed.

How You Retrieve an Attachment Depends on the Email Package   If you send messages with attachments to users who do not have Outlook or Microsoft's Outlook Express, how they retrieve the file attachment will vary. Some email packages do not show the attachment as an icon, but save the attachment directly to a file after the email message is downloaded. If you send attachments to someone and they are having trouble retrieving them, they should consult the help system of their particular email client.

To attach a file to a message, follow these steps:

1. In the Message window, choose Insert, File or click the Insert File button on the toolbar. The Insert File dialog box appears (see Figure 9.1).

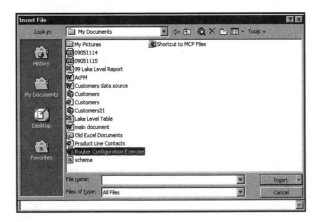

FIGURE 9.1   Select the file you want to attach to a message.

2. From the Look In drop-down list, choose the drive and folder that contains the file you want to attach.

3. Using the Files of Type drop-down list, choose the file type, such as Excel or Word.

4. Select the file you want to attach.

5. Click OK to insert the file into the message.

Figure 9.2 shows a file inserted as an attachment.

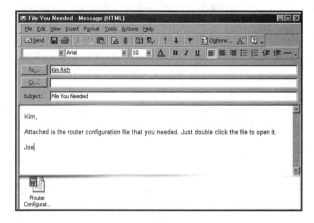

FIGURE 9.2   The recipient can double-click the icon to open the file.

 Large Files Take Time   Sending an extremely large file can take a great deal of time depending on your connection speed. You may want to compress large files using products like WinZip or PKZip. These compression tools allow you to compress the size of attachments. However, the receivers of your messages will also need these tools if they are going to uncompress your attachments.

UNDERSTANDING ATTACHMENT FORMAT TYPES

When you attach a file to an email message, it is coded in a special way so that the information remains intact when sent as part of the email message. Two of the most popular coding systems for attachments are *MIME* (Multipurpose Internet Mail Extension) and *UUEncoding*.

MIME   This coding scheme places a header in the email message just before the information contained in the attached file. This lets the recipient's email client recognize which part of the sent message is the message text and which part is the attachment. Some online services and email packages have a problem decoding MIME attached files.

UUEncoding   One of the most popular coding schemes. Most email packages can recognize and decode UUEncoded messages.

Check with Online Service Users   Some online services, such as America Online, have restrictions on the size of an email that their mail server will accept. You should check with AOL or other service users before you send them files with large attachments to see if they have any special requirements.

Outlook enables you to select either MIME or UUEncoding as your default attachment format. To select the attachment coding system, follow these steps:

1. Click Tools, Options; the Options dialog box appears.

2. Click the Internet E-mail tab. Select either the MIME or the UUENCODE radio button. UUENCODE is embraced by most

email clients and should be your choice unless you know that you are specifically sending to individuals who use a client that embraces the MIME format.

3. After making your selection, click OK.

ATTACHING OUTLOOK ITEMS

In addition to attaching files from other programs, you can also attach an Outlook item to a message. An Outlook item can be any document saved in one of your personal folders, including a calendar, contacts, journal, notes, tasks, and so on. You can attach an Outlook item in the same manner you attach a file.

Follow these steps to attach an Outlook item:

1. In the Message window, choose Insert, Item. The Insert Item dialog box appears.

2. From the Look In list, choose the folder containing the item you want to include in the message.

3. Select from the items that appear in the Items list (see Figure 9.3). To select multiple adjacent items, hold down the Shift key and click the first and last desired items; to select multiple non-adjacent items, hold down the Ctrl key and click the items.

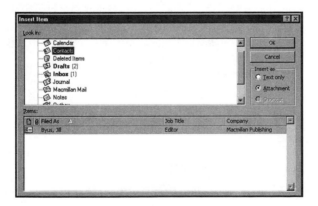

FIGURE 9.3 Select items from any folder in Outlook such as a contact's information from the Contacts folder.

4. In the Insert As area, choose from the following option buttons:

Text Only   Inserts the file as text into the message; if your file is not saved as an ASCII or other text-only file, do not use this option.

Attachment   Inserts an icon representing the document. The actual file follows the message to the recipient; the recipient saves it as his or her own copy.

Shortcut   Inserts a Windows 98/NT shortcut icon into the text. This option can only be used if the file is stored on a network drive from which the recipient can easily access it through a shortcut.

Text Only Is Only for Text!   If you try to insert a file from Word, Excel, or another application as Text Only, you'll end up with a lot of *garbage* characters in the text. That's because these programs' files contain special formatting codes. The only time you will use Text Only is when you export the data from its native program into a text-only file first.

5. Click OK; Outlook inserts the selected items in your message.

It Doesn't Work Without Outlook   If the recipient doesn't have Outlook on his computer, he will not be able to view the attached item. If you know the recipient doesn't have the program, you'll need to cut and paste the data into the message or simply retype it.

INSERTING AN OBJECT

Just as you can insert an object—a spreadsheet, chart, drawing presentation, media clip, clip art, WordArt, and so on—in any Windows

application that supports *OLE*, you can also insert an object into your
Outlook items, such as your calendar or task list. Inserting a file in a message, as discussed earlier, is the equivalent of inserting an object into one
of the other Outlook items.

 OLE (Object Linking and Embedding)   A method of
exchanging and sharing data between applications;
OLE is supported by most Windows applications and
all Microsoft programs.

You can insert an existing object into an Outlook item, or you can create
an object within a message using the source application. For example,
you could create an Excel chart within your message using Excel's features through OLE.

When you send a message with an attached object, the object travels
with the message to the recipient. As long as the recipient has the application on his computer (or applicable viewer), he can open the object and
view it.

For more information about OLE, see Lesson 22, "Sharing Data with
Office Applications."

To attach an existing object to an appointment or task in the calendar, follow these steps:

1. Click the Calendar icon in the Outlook bar. Double-click an
   appointment or task on the task list. Position the insertion point
   in the appointment or task text box and choose Insert, Object.
   The Insert Object dialog box appears.

2. Choose the Create from File option (see Figure 9.4).

3. In the File text box, enter the path and the name of the file you
   want to insert. (You can use the Browse button and the resulting
   dialog box to find the file if you want.)

4. Click OK. Outlook inserts the object into the Outlook item.

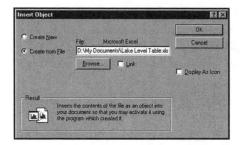

FIGURE 9.4   Insert an object to send with a message.

To edit an object, double-click within the frame, and the source application opens from within Outlook. Note that you'll still see your Outlook item and Outlook toolbars; however, you'll also see tools associated with the object's source application, which you can use to edit the object. Figure 9.5 shows an Excel spreadsheet object within a Calendar appointment. Notice the Excel toolbar and icons appear at the top of the Outlook window because the OLE object you have double-clicked is an Excel object and requires Excel's capabilities for editing.

When you double-click an object that is embedded in an Outlook item, you can resize the object to suit your needs. First select it, and a frame appears with eight small black boxes (called *handles*) on the corners and along the sides. To resize the object, position the mouse pointer over one of the black handles; the mouse pointer becomes a two-headed arrow. Click and drag the handle to resize the object.

For more information about working with the calendar and appointments see Lesson 15, "Using the Calendar."

Toolbar added for Excel

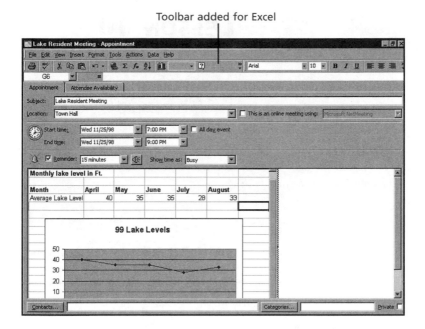

FIGURE 9.5   Edit the object from within your Outlook message.

In this lesson, you learned to attach a file and other items to a message. You also learned to insert an object in an Outlook item. In the next lesson you learn to organize messages.

LESSON 10
ORGANIZING MESSAGES

In this lesson you learn to save a draft, view sent items, create folders, and move items to the new folder.

SAVING A DRAFT

Suppose you start a message, but you are called away or need to do something else before you can finish it. You don't have to cancel the message and start over again later; you can save the message in the Draft folder and then open it later to complete it.

To save a draft, follow these steps:

1. In the Message window, click the Close button. A dialog box will appear asking if you want to save changes, as shown in Figure 10.1.

FIGURE 10.1 Click Yes to save the message in the Drafts folder for later completion.

2. Click Yes. Outlook places the current message in the Drafts Folder.

To open the message and continue working on it at another time, follow these steps:

1. Click the Drafts folder icon in the My Shortcuts group on the Outlook Bar, or choose Drafts from the Folders list.

2. Double-click the message to open it. At the top of the Message tab, you'll see a reminder that this message has not been sent.

3. Continue your work on the message. If you need to store it again before you're finished, click the Close button or choose File, Close. The message remains in the Drafts folder until you move it or send it.

4. When you're finished, click the Send button to send the message.

Create an Outlook Bar Icon for Drafts If you would like to place a Drafts folder icon on the Outlook bar when you are in the Outlook Shortcuts group, open the Folders list, pin the Folders list down, and then right-click the Draft folder. On the shortcut menu that appears, select Add to Outlook Bar. An icon will appear on the Outlook bar for the Drafts folder.

VIEWING SENT ITEMS AND CHANGING DEFAULTS

By default, Outlook saves a copy of all mail messages you send. It keeps these copies in the Sent Items folder, which is part of the Mail group of the Outlook bar. You can view a list of sent items at any time, and you can open any message in that list to review its contents.

VIEWING SENT ITEMS

To view sent items, follow these steps:

1. In the Outlook bar, choose the My Shortcuts group.

Save Time   You can select the Sent Items folder from
the Folder list instead of following steps 1–3.

2. If necessary, scroll to the Sent Items folder.

3. Click the Sent Items icon, and Outlook displays a list of the contents of that folder. Figure 10.2 shows the Sent Items list. All messages you send remain in the Sent Items folder until you delete or move them.

4. (Optional) To view a sent item, double-click it to open it. When you finish with it, click the Close (X) button.

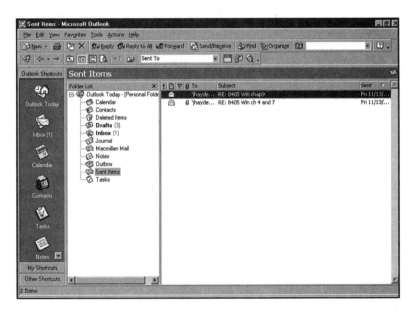

FIGURE 10.2   You can open any sent message by double-clicking it.

CHANGING DEFAULTS FOR SENT ITEMS

You can control whether or not Outlook saves copies of your sent messages (this is also true for unsent messages). To change the default setting for the Sent Items folder, follow these steps:

1. Choose Tools, Options, and the Options dialog box appears.

2. Make sure that the Preferences tab is selected on the dialog box.

3. Click the E-mail Options button. The E-mail Options dialog box appears (see Figure 10.3). This dialog box allows you to toggle several email-related features on and off:

   - **Close Original Message on Reply or Forward**   When this is checked, the message you currently have open will be closed when you reply to it or forward it. If this setting is unchecked, Outlook leaves the message window open.

   - **Save Copies of Messages in Sent Items Folder**   When this is checked, Outlook saves copies of all sent messages to the specified folder. (When the check box is empty, no copies of messages are saved automatically.)

   - **Automatically Save Unsent Messages**   When this is checked, Outlook saves your unfinished messages every three minutes, placing them in the Drafts folder. If you remove the check box from this feature, drafts are not automatically saved.

   - **Close Original Message on Reply or Forward**   When this is checked, the message you currently have open will be closed when you reply to it or forward it. If this setting is unchecked, Outlook leaves the message window open.

   - **Display a Notification Message When New E-mail Arrives**   When this is checked, a message appears in the Outlook window that new mail has arrived.

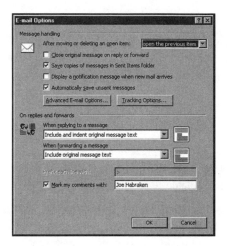

FIGURE 10.3   The E-mail Options dialog box gives you control over a number of features related to sending and receiving email messages.

The E-mail Options dialog box also gives you control over several other features related to the management of your email.

- **Advanced E-mail Options button**   This button opens the Advanced E-mail Options dialog box. Most of the feature controls in the Advanced E-mail Options dialog box take the form of either check boxes or drop-down boxes. This dialog box allows you to control:

    The folder that unsent messages are sent to

    How often to save unsent messages

    Whether or not to save forwarded messages

    The default importance and sensitivity for outgoing messages

- **Tracking Options button**   This button opens the Tracking Options dialog box where you can toggle on and off the following features:

  Tell me when all messages have been delivered.

  Tell me when all messages have been read.

  Delete receipts and blank responses after processing.

To close the E-Mail Options dialog box, click OK.

 Too Much Mail!   If you save all the mail you receive and send, you may accumulate so much mail that you run the risk of running out of disk space. You can and should periodically delete mail from the Sent Items folder by selecting the mail and pressing the Delete key; you'll also need to remove the deleted mail from the Deleted Items folder. See Lesson 7, "Working with Received Mail," for more information. Alternatively, you can create an archive file of the messages you've sent. The archive enables you to save items on disk or elsewhere on the system. See Lesson 23, "Archiving Items," for details.

CREATING FOLDERS

You'll probably want to organize your mail in various folders to make storing items and finding them more efficient. You can create folders within Outlook that make it easier to manage your mail and other items in Outlook.

To create a folder, follow these steps:

1. Choose File, New, Folder. The Create New Folder dialog box appears (see Figure 10.4).

FIGURE 10.4   Create folders to organize your mail and other items.

2. In the Name text box, enter a name for the folder.

3. Click the Folder Contains drop-down arrow, and choose the type of items the folder will store: Mail, Appointments, Contact, Journal, Note, or Task.

4. Double-click the folder in which you want to create the new folder. You can, for example, make the new folder a subfolder of Personal Folders so that it appears in lists with all of the Outlook folders. Or you might want to make it a subfolder of Sent Mail.

5. Click OK to close the dialog box. A message box will appear asking if you want a shortcut icon created for the new folder on the Outlook bar. Click Yes if you want the shortcut.

The new folder appears on the Outlook bar and in the Folder List.

 Add Folder Later   Even if you choose not to add the folder to the Outlook bar when you create the folder, you can add it later. You simply right-click the folder in the folder list and select Add to Outlook Bar from the shortcut menu that appears.

I Want to Delete a Folder! If you added a folder by accident or you change your mind about a folder you've added, you can delete it from Outlook. To delete a folder, select it and then choose File, Folder, Delete *foldername*. You also can rename, move, and/or copy the folder using the commands in the secondary menu that appears when you choose File, Folder.

MOVING ITEMS TO ANOTHER FOLDER

You can move items from one folder in Outlook to another; for example, you can create a folder to store all messages pertaining to a specific account or report. You can easily move those messages to the new folder and open them later for reference purposes. You also can forward, reply, copy, delete, and archive any items you move from one folder to another.

To move an item to another folder, follow these steps:

1. From the Inbox, or any Outlook folder, open the message you want to move.

2. Choose Edit, Move to Folder. The Move Items dialog box appears (see Figure 10.5).

FIGURE 10.5 Choose the folder in which you want to store the message or messages.

3. In the list of folders, select the folder to which you want to move the message.

4. Choose OK. When you close the message, Outlook stores it in the designated folder.

Quick Move   You can quickly move an unopened message by dragging it from the open folder in which it resides to any folder icon in the Outlook bar.

You can open the message at any time by opening the folder from the Outlook bar and double-clicking the message. After opening it, you can forward, send, print, or otherwise manipulate the message as you would any message.

You should also keep in mind that you can also copy messages from one folder to another. Copying a message or messages works very much like moving a message or message. To start the copy process, select the message or messages you want to copy and then choose Edit, Copy to Folder. Select the folder you want to copy to in the Copy Items dialog box.

Manage Messages with the Organizer Tool and Rules Wizard   Two great tools for helping you manage your messages are the Organize tool and the Rules Wizard. Both features are covered in Lesson 8, "Managing Electronic Mail."

In this lesson you learned to save a draft, view sent items, create folders, and move items to a folder. In the next lesson you learn to set various Outlook mail options.

LESSON 11
SETTING MAIL
OPTIONS

In this lesson you learn to set options for messages and delivery, and for tracking messages.

CUSTOMIZING OPTIONS

Outlook provides options that enable you to mark any message with priority status so that the recipient knows you need a quick response, or with a sensitivity rating so your words cannot be changed by anyone after the message is sent. With other options, you can enable the recipients of your message to vote on an issue by including voting buttons in your message and having the replies sent to a specific location.

You also can set delivery options. For example, you can schedule the delivery of a message for a specified delivery time or date if you don't want to send it right now.

Recognizing Priority Flags Not all email packages will recognize the priority flags you place on messages you send. These priority flags work ideally in a network situation, where Outlook is the email client for all users (this works particularly well for networks using Microsoft Exchange Server as the email service). Results will vary for Internet email. Microsoft Outlook Express, for example, recognizes Outlook priority flags on messages sent as Internet email.

To set message options, open a new Untitled - Message window and click the Options button on the toolbar. As you can see in Figure 11.1, the Message Options dialog box is separated into four areas. The next four subsections discuss each group of options in detail.

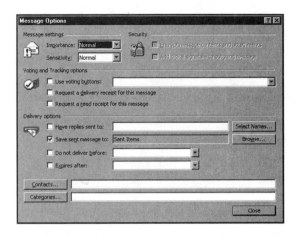

FIGURE 11.1   Use the Message Options settings to govern how your message is sent.

MESSAGE SETTINGS

In the Message Settings area, set any of the following options for your message:

- Click the Importance drop-down arrow and choose a priority level of Low, Normal, or High from the list. (Alternatively, you could click the Importance High or Importance Low button on the message's toolbar when you compose the message.) When importance isn't specified, the message is given Normal Importance.

- Click the Sensitivity drop-down arrow and choose one of the following options:

    Normal   Use this option to indicate that the message contents are standard, or customary.

Personal   Use this option to suggest that the message contents are of a personal nature.

Private   Use this option to prevent the message from being edited (text changes, copy, paste, and so on) after you send it.

Confidential   Use this option to indicate that the message contents are restricted or private.

You Can Mark All Messages As Private   You can mark all your new messages as private automatically. Choose Tools, Options and then click the E-mail Options button. On the E-mail Options dialog box, click the Advanced E-mail Options button. Use the Sensitivity drop-down box at the bottom of Advance E-mail Options dialog box to set the default sensitivity for all your new email messages.

Outlook also supplies you with two security options. You can choose to encrypt the contents and attachments of a message: click the Encrypt Contents and Attachments check box next to the Security icon. You can also add a digital signature to the message that verifies you are the sender: click the Add Digital Signature to Outgoing Message check box.

Encryption   Messages are coded so that they remain secure until the recipient opens them. The recipient is able to decode the message because he or she is identified by Digital ID.

Digital Signature   A Digital ID that is electronically stamped on messages that you send.

Before you can use the encryption and digital signature features in Outlook 2000, you must obtain a Digital ID, which is also often referred to as a certificate. Digital IDs are issued by an independent certifying authority. Microsoft's certifying authority of choice is VeriSign Digital ID. You can obtain, download, and install your Digital ID from VeriSign by following the steps on their Web page at **http://digitalid.verisign.com/**.

VOTING AND TRACKING OPTIONS

The Voting and Tracking Options allow you to control special features like voting buttons (these allow recipients of the message to reply with a click of the mouse) and supply you with the means to track the receipt of your message. You must be using the corporate email installation to take advantage of Voting buttons (see Lesson 3 for more information on the differences between the two different Outlook installations).

- Select the Use Voting Buttons check box to add the default choices (Approve and Reject) to your message. You can also add Yes and No choices or Yes, No, and Maybe choices. If you want to provide other choices, enter your own text in the text box.

- Select Tell Me When This Message Has Been Delivered to receive an email notification that the message has been received by the recipient.

- Select Tell Me When This Message Has Been Read to receive email confirmation that the message has been opened by the recipient.

DELIVERY OPTIONS

In addition to voting and tracking options, you can set certain delivery options, such as having replies sent to individuals you select. You can also choose a folder where a copy of the message will be saved, or schedule the time of the delivery. In the Delivery Options area of the Message Options dialog box, choose any of the following check boxes:

- Choose the Have Replies Sent To check box and specify in the text box the person to whom you want the replies sent. You can use the Select Names button to view the Address Book and choose a name if you want.

- Select the Save Sent Message To check box to save your message to the Sent Items folder by default. Or specify another folder to save the message in, using the Browse button and the resulting dialog box if necessary to locate the folder.

- Select the Do Not Deliver Before option to specify a delivery date. Click the down arrow in the text box beside the option to display a calendar on which you can select the day.

- Select the Expires After check box to include a day, date, and time of expiration. You can click the down arrow in the text box to display a calendar from which you can choose a date, or you can enter the date and time yourself.

CATEGORIES

Outlook enables you to assign messages to certain categories—such as Business, Goals, Hot Contacts, Phone Calls, and so on. You set the category for a message in the Categories dialog box.

 Categories Categories offer a way of organizing messages to make them easier to find, sort, print, and manage. For example, to find all of the items in one category, choose Tools, Find Items. Click the More Choices tab, choose Categories, and check the category for which you're searching.

To assign a category, follow these steps:

1. In the Message Options dialog box, click the Categories button. The Categories dialog box appears (see Figure 11.2).

2. To assign an existing category, select the category or categories that best suit your message from the Available Categories list. To assign a new category, enter a new category in the Item(s) Belong to These Categories text box, and then click the Add to List button.

FIGURE 11.2   Organize your messages with categories.

3. Click OK to close the Categories dialog box and return to the Message Options dialog box.

When you have set all the options for the current message, click the Close button to close the Message Options box and return to the message window.

USING MESSAGE FLAGS

A message flag enables you to mark a message as important, either as a reminder for yourself or as a signal to the message's recipient. When you send a message flag, a red flag icon appears in the recipient's message list, and Outlook adds text at the top of the message telling which type of flag you are sending. In addition, you can add a due date to the flag, and that date appears at the top of the message.

The following list outlines the types of flags you can send in Outlook:

Call	No Response Necessary
Do Not Forward	Read
Follow Up	Reply
For Your Information	Reply to All
Forward	Review

To use a message flag, follow these steps:

1. In the Message window, click Actions, Flag For Follow Up. The Flag for Follow Up dialog box appears (see Figure 11.3).

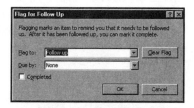

FIGURE 11.3   Flag a message to show its importance.

2. Click the Flag To drop-down arrow and choose the flag text you want to add to the message.

3. Click the Reminder drop-down arrow enter a date in the text box.

4. Click OK to return to the Message window.

Figure 11.4 shows the Inbox and with a few flagged messages.

 View the Message Header   You can view just the header of a message to allow you more message text room if you want to hide the Cc, Bcc, and Subject lines. Choose View, Message Header to show only the To text box and any flag text; select View, Message Header again to redisplay the Cc, Bcc, and Subject fields.

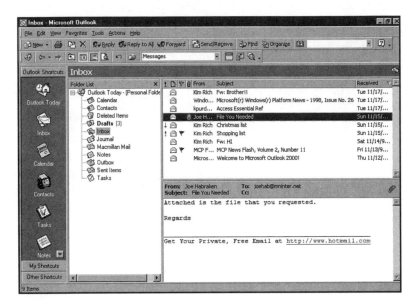

FIGURE 11.4   Flagged messages in the Inbox folder. To view the type of flag attached, open the message.

Marking messages with the Follow Up flag is a great way to remind yourself that you need to attend to a particular issue. Flagging messages for your email recipients helps them prioritize responses, so that you receive the needed reply within a particular time frame.

When you double-click on a flagged message and open it in a message window, the flag type appears at the top of the message, just above the From: box. Viewing the flag type on the message provides you with a quick reminder as to what your next action will be regarding the particular message (see Figure 11.5).

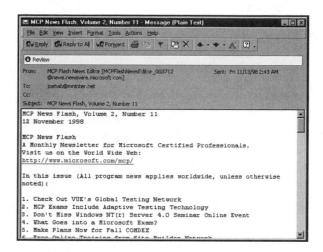

FIGURE 11.5   The message flag provides you with a quick reminder of what action you want to take in relation to the currently selected message.

In this lesson you learned to set options for messages and delivery, and for tracking messages. In the next lesson you learn to attach items to messages.

LESSON 12

USING THE CONTACT AND PERSONAL ADDRESS BOOKS

In this lesson you learn to use Outlook's Contact and address books with your email.

USING THE POSTOFFICE ADDRESS LIST

If you use Outlook as your email client on a corporate mail server (meaning you have installed Outlook using the corporate mail configuration), many of the messages you send will be to coworkers on that same network. The email addresses for these people will be determined by your network administrator. Even if you do use Outlook as a corporate client, you can set it up to also serve as your Internet email program (see Lesson 3, "Understanding the Outlook Configurations," for more information on the setup options).

 Internet Email Internet email is sent over the Internet by means of a modem or your corporate network. Internet email addresses usually take the form of *username@company.com*.

If you use corporate email, such as Microsoft Mail, or connect to Microsoft Exchange Server to communicate with your coworkers, all of the email names within your organization usually appear on the Postoffice Address List created by your system's mail administrator. Whenever you want to send or forward an email, you can select the recipients from that list instead of typing in their names manually (or entering them in one of the other Outlook Address books or Contact lists). Whether or not you have access to the Postoffice Address List will depend on your permissions and rights on the network that you are connected to. If you have a question, see your network administrator.

If you've installed Outlook for Internet Only email, you will not have a Postoffice Address List as one of the possibilities in the drop-down list when you open the Address Book dialog box.

Post Office   A directory, usually located on the network server, that contains a mailbox for each email user. When someone sends a message, that message is filed in the recipient's mailbox until the recipient receives the mail and copies, moves, or deletes it.

Postoffice Address List   A list of everyone who has a mailbox in the post office; it's controlled by the mail administrator.

Mail Administrator   The person who manages the email post office. (This person might also be the network administrator, but it doesn't necessarily have to be the same person.)

To use the Postoffice Address List, choose Tools, Address Book or click the Address Book button on the toolbar. The Address Book dialog box appears, as shown in Figure 12.1.

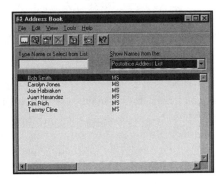

FIGURE 12.1 View the Postoffice Address List.

The following list outlines some of the ways in which you might use the Address List:

- To view more details about any entry in the Address Book dialog box (which contains the Postoffice Address List), double-click the person's name or click the Properties button on the toolbar. The person's Properties dialog box appears, with his or her name, address type, Postoffice name, and network type listed on the Address (1) tab. Click OK to close this dialog box and return to the Address Book dialog box.

- Click the Properties button on the toolbar and choose the Business tab in the person's Properties dialog box to view his or her phone number, office, or department, and any notes or comments that have been added to the description. Click OK to close this dialog box and return to the Address Book dialog box.

- To send a message to someone listed in the Address Book, select the name from the Address List and choose File, New Message. See Lesson 6 for more information.

- If you cannot find a particular name in the list, you can search for it. Choose Tools, Find or click the Find button, and then enter the name for which you're searching in the Find Name text box. Click OK to start the search.

If your corporation or organization uses Microsoft Exchange Server as its mail server, you can use Outlook as the email client, as you can for other email systems like Microsoft Mail or Internet mail. If you are connected to a Microsoft Exchange Server (the mail component of Microsoft NT Server), an additional list for mail addresses will appear in the Address Book drop-down list. You will have access to a list called *Global Address List*. This list, like the Post Office Address list described earlier for Microsoft Mail Postoffice groups, is controlled and maintained by your Network Administrator.

USING THE PERSONAL ADDRESS BOOK

The Personal Address Book contains the names and email addresses of people you contact frequently. You may want to include coworkers from your department, or even people from outside your office (whom you contact by using Internet addresses).

 The Contacts Book You may notice Contacts in the list of address books; this book contains entries you create in your Contacts list. For more information about the Contacts list, see Lesson 13.

 No Personal Address Book Is Listed? If you do not see a Personal Address Book in the Address Book dialog box, you can easily add it to your resources. Close the address book and choose Tools, Services. In the Services tab of the dialog box, choose the Add button, and from the list, choose the Personal Address Book; then choose OK. Close the Services dialog box and open the address book again; you'll see the Personal Address Book in the list.

To add names to the Personal Address Book, follow these steps:

1. Choose Tools, Address Book, or click the Address Book button on the toolbar. The Address Book dialog box appears (refer to Figure 12.1).

2. To add name(s) from the Postoffice Address List, select the name(s) and click the Add to Personal Address Book button on the toolbar or choose File, Add to Personal Address Book. The name(s) remain on the Postoffice Address List, but Outlook copies them to your Personal Address Book as well. You can also add names from the Contacts list to the Personal Address Book in this manner.

3. To view your Personal Address Book, select the Show Names from the drop-down list and choose Personal Address Book. The list changes to display those names you've added to your personal address list, but the dialog box looks the same.

4. To add a completely new address to your Personal Address Book, click the New Entry button or choose File, New Entry. The New Entry dialog box appears (see Figure 12.2).

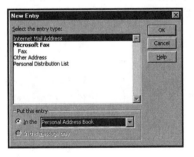

FIGURE 12.2   Choose a source for your new entry.

5. In the Select the Entry Type list, choose from the available options. The options you see will depend on the information systems installed on your network; for example, Microsoft Mail, Internet Mail, or some other service may be available (such as Microsoft Fax). You can add an address entry that corresponds with one of the available information systems.

Additionally, you can choose to add one of the following two items:

Personal Distribution List   Use this to create one address entry for a group of recipients. When you send mail to the list name, everyone on the list receives the message. You might use this option for grouping department heads, for example.

Other Address   Choose this option to add one new recipient at a time. You can enter a name, email address, and email type for each entry. In addition, you can enter business addresses and phone numbers, and you can add notes and comments to the entry. Use this entry for Internet addresses, for example.

6. When you're done working in your Personal Address Book, close the window by choosing File, Close. You return to the Outlook Inbox.

IMPORTING ADDRESS BOOKS AND CONTACT LISTS

If you are migrating from another personal information manager or email client and want to import your address book or contacts list, Outlook contains a number of different conversion filters for this purpose. Outlook even provides you with an Import/Export Wizard that walks you through the steps of importing address lists and address books from these other software packages.

To start the Outlook Import/Export Wizard, follow these steps:

1. Click File, Import and Export. The Outlook Import and Export Wizard opens (see Figure 12.3).

2. On the first wizard screen, click Import from Another Program or File, Next. Conversion filters are available for popular personal information managers like Lotus Organizer and Sidekick. You can also import information from Microsoft Access and Microsoft Schedule Plus among others. Also any program that can save your former address book as a delimited file allows you to import the information into Outlook.

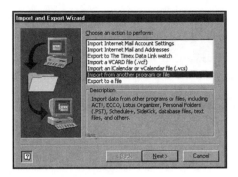

FIGURE **12.3**   The Import and Export Wizard walks you through the process of importing your old address books.

Delimited File   Most database programs and personal information managers can save address books in a delimited format. This means that spaces or tabs are placed between the different fields of information. Saving an address book as a delimited file makes it possible to import the information into a number of different software packages that do not share the same file format as the software you are importing from.

3. Choose the program or file type that you want to use to import the address book, and then click Next.

4. The next wizard screen asks you to type in the name of the file you are importing or to locate the file on your computer using the Browse button. After you have selected the file, you can select one of the following option buttons:

   Replace Duplicates with Items Imported

   Allow Duplicates to Be Created

   Do Not Import Duplicate Items

5. After making your selections, click Next.

6. The next screen asks you to select the folder in which you want to place the new information. Because you are importing an Address Book, you will want to place the imported data into your Contacts folder. Click Next to continue.

7. The last screen asks you to match up the fields in the imported data with fields available in a typical Contacts form, such as Name, Address, Phone Number, Fax, and so on. Click the Map Custom Fields button to do this. The Map Custom Fields dialog box appears.

8. Drag a field from the import file box to the Outlook Contact box. Match fields that contain the same kind of data. For example, if the import file contains a field for Phone, and you want this information to appear in the Contact Business phone field, drag the Phone field from the import box and place it next to the Business phone field in the Contacts box (see Figure 12.4).

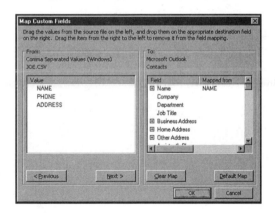

FIGURE 12.4   Match the fields in the import file with the fields in Contacts.

When you have completed matching the fields, click OK. You return to the final Wizard screen. Click Finish. The contact information from the import file will be placed in your Outlook Contact folder.

In this lesson, you learned to use the address book with your email and import address books from other software programs. In the next lesson, you learn to create a Contacts list.

LESSON 13

CREATING A CONTACTS LIST

In this lesson you learn to create and view a Contacts list, and to send mail to someone on your Contacts list.

CREATING A NEW CONTACT

You use the Contacts folder to create, store, and access your Contacts list. You can enter any or all of the following information about each contact:

- Name
- Job title
- Company name
- Address (Street, City, State, Zip, and Country)
- Phone (business, home, business fax, mobile)
- Email address
- Web page address
- Comments, notes, or descriptions
- Categories

 Contact In Outlook, a contact is any person or company for which you've entered a name, address, phone number, or other information. You can communicate with a contact in Outlook by sending an email message, scheduling a meeting, sending a letter, and so on.

You also can edit the information at any time, add new contacts, or delete contacts from the list. To open the Contacts folder and create a new contact, follow these steps:

1. To open the Contacts folder, click the Contacts shortcut on the Outlook bar. The Contacts folder opens.

2. To create a new contact, select Actions, New Contact, or simply click the New Contact button on the Standard toolbar. The Contact dialog box appears, with the General tab displayed (see Figure 13.1).

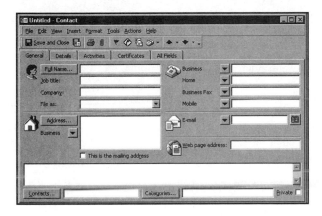

FIGURE 13.1   You can enter as much or as little information about each contact as you need.

3. Enter the contact's name in the Name text box. If you want to add more detailed information for the name, click the Full Name button to display the Check Full Name dialog box, and then enter the contact's title and full name (including first, middle, and last names) and any suffix you want to include. Click OK to close the Check Full Name dialog box and return to the Contact dialog box.

4. Press the Tab key and then enter the client's company name and job title. This information is optional.

5. In the File As drop-down box, enter or select the method by which you want to file your contact's names. You can choose

last name first or first name first, or you can enter your own filing system, such as by company or state.

> **Keep It Simple**   The default filing method for con-
> tacts is last name first, which makes it easy to quickly
> find the contact when you need it.

6. Enter the address in the Address box and choose whether the
   address is Business, Home, or Other. Alternatively, you can
   click the Address button to enter the street, city, state, ZIP code,
   and country in specified areas instead of all within the text
   block. You can add a second address (say, the Home address) if
   you want. Address information is optional.

7. In the Phone drop-down lists, choose the type of phone number—Business, Callback, Car, Home Fax, ISDN, Pager, and so
   on—and then enter the number. You can enter up to 19 numbers
   in each of the four drop-down boxes in the Phone area of the
   dialog box.

8. You can enter up to three email addresses in the E-mail text box;
   in the Web Page Address text box, enter the address for the company or contact's URL on the World Wide Web.

> **If You Have More Than One Email Address for a**
> **Contact**   When you place more than one phone num-
> ber or email address in a drop-down list, the first
> number or address in the list serves as the default. For
> example, when emailing a contact, the first email
> address in the list will serve as the default and be
> placed in the To box on the new message. If you want
> to use a different email address for the contact,
> double-click the contact's name in the Message To
> box, and select one of the other email addresses in
> the contact's Properties box. When you want to call a
> contact for whom you have multiple numbers, a drop-
> down list appears in the New Call dialog box and
> allows you to choose the appropriate number.

URL Stands for Uniform Resource Locator, and simply means the address for a Web page on the World Wide Web. A typical URL would be written http://www.*companyname*.com, such as http://www.mcp.com.

9. In the comment text box, enter any descriptions, comments, or other pertinent information you want. Then select or enter a category to classify the contact.

10. After you have completed entering the new contact information, click the Save and Close button to return to the Contacts folder. You can also save the new contact by opening the File menu and choosing one of the following commands:

> **Save** Saves the record and closes the Contact dialog box.

> **Save and New** Saves the record and clears the Contact dialog box so you can enter a new contact.

You can edit the information about a contact at any time by double-clicking the contact's name in the Contacts list; this displays the contact's information window. Alternatively, you can click within the information listed below a contact's name (such as the phone number or address) to position the insertion point in the text, and then delete or enter text. Press Enter to complete the modifications you've made and move to the next contact in the list.

VIEWING THE CONTACTS LIST

By default, you see the contacts in an Address Cards view. The information you see displays the contact's name and other data such as addresses and phone numbers. The contact's company name, job title, and comments, however, are not displayed by default. Figure 13.2 shows the Contacts list in the default Address Cards view.

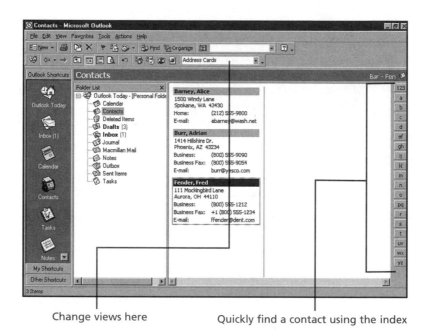

Change views here   Quickly find a contact using the index

FIGURE 13.2   View your contacts in Address Cards view.

You can use the horizontal scrollbar to view more contacts, or you can click a letter in the index to display contacts beginning with that letter in the first column of the list.

Do I Save View Settings?   Depending on the changes you make to a view, Outlook might display the Save View Settings dialog box to ask if you want to save the view settings before you switch to a different view. If you choose to save the current settings, Outlook lets you name the view and adds that view to the current view list. If you choose to discard the current settings, your modifications to the view will be lost. If you choose to update the view, your modifications are saved with that view.

You can change how you view the contacts in the list by choosing one of these options from the current view drop-down list on the Standard toolbar:

- **Address Cards**   Displays File As names (last name first, first name last, and so on), addresses, and phone numbers of the contacts, depending on the amount of information you've entered in a card format.

- **Detailed Address Cards**   Displays File As name, full name, job title, company, addresses, phone numbers, email addresses, categories, and comments in a card format.

- **Phone List**   Displays full name, job title, company, File As name, department, phone numbers, and categories in a table, organizing each entry horizontally in rows and columns.

- **By Category**   Displays contacts in rows by categories. The information displayed is the same as what's displayed in a phone list.

- **By Company**   Displays contacts in rows, grouped by their company. The information displayed is the same as what's displayed in a phone list.

- **By Location**   Displays contacts grouped by country. The information displayed is the same as what's displayed in a phone list.

- **By Follow Up Flag**   Displays contacts grouped by follow-up flags. The view also displays the due date for the follow-up that you specified when you marked the contact with a flag.

Use the Letter Tabs to View Contacts Alphabetically If you have a large number of contacts in your Contacts list, you can quickly jump to just the contacts who have a last name that begins with a letter or letter range of the alphabet. Click on the appropriate letter tab on the right side of the Contacts list to view particular contacts.

COMMUNICATING WITH A CONTACT

You can send messages to any of your contacts, arrange meetings, assign tasks, or even send a letter to a contact from within Outlook. To communicate with a contact, make sure you're in the Contacts folder. You do not need to open the specific contact's information window to perform any of the following procedures.

SENDING MESSAGES

To send a message to a contact, you must make sure you've entered an email address in the General tab of the Contact dialog box for that particular contact. If Outlook cannot locate the mailing address, it displays a message dialog box (see Figure 13.3).

FIGURE 13.3   Outlook cannot send the email until you place the needed address in the To: box of the New Message dialog box.

 To send a message from the Contacts folder, select the contact and choose Actions, New Message to Contact. In the Untitled - Message dialog box, enter the subject and message and set any options you want. When you're ready to send the message, click the Send button. For more information about sending mail, see Lesson 6, "Creating Mail."

SCHEDULING A MEETING WITH A CONTACT

To schedule a meeting with a contact, the contact must have a valid email address. If no address is listed for the contact, Outlook notifies you with a message box and enables you to enter an address within the message dialog box. If the listed address is not found, Outlook responds with the Check Names dialog box, as described in the previous section.

To schedule a meeting with a contact, select the contact and choose Actions, New Meeting with Contact. The Untitled - Meeting dialog box appears. Enter the subject, location, time and date, and other information you need to schedule the meeting, and then notify the contact by sending an invitation. For more information about scheduling meetings, see Lesson 14, "Planning a Meeting."

ASSIGNING A TASK TO A CONTACT

Tasks are assigned through email. Therefore, you must enter a valid email address for the contact before you can assign him or her a task.

To assign a task to a contact, select the contact and choose Actions, New Task for Contact. The Task dialog box appears. Enter the subject, due date, status, and other information, and then send the task to the contact. For detailed information about assigning tasks, see Lesson 16, "Creating a Task List."

SENDING A LETTER TO A CONTACT

Outlook uses the Microsoft Word Letter Wizard to help you create a letter to send to a contact. Within the Word Wizard, you follow directions as they appear onscreen to complete the text of the letter.

To send a letter to the contact, select the contact in the Contacts folder and choose Actions, New Letter to Contact. Word opens the Letter Wizard onscreen. The Letter Wizard helps you format and complete the letter (see Figure 13.4). You can click the Office Assistant button if you need additional help. All you have to do is follow the directions and make your choices.

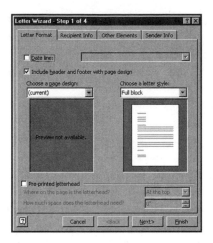

FIGURE 13.4   Use Word's Letter Wizard to create a letter to a contact.

CALLING A CONTACT

Another obvious way to communicate with a contact is over the telephone. Outlook makes it easy for you to make a phone call to a contact and in fact will dial the phone number for you.

For Outlook to dial the phone call for you, you must have a modem hooked to your computer that can dial out for you. On a network, if you have access to a network modem pool, you can also dial out using your computer, if the line you dial out on can also be accessed by your telephone.

To initiate a phone call to a contact, select the contact in the Contacts list and follow these steps:

1. Select Actions, Call Contact, and then select the appropriate phone number from the cascading menu that appears (all the phone numbers including business, home, and fax for the selected contact will appear) or simply click the Autodialer button on the Standard toolbar and select the appropriate phone number from the drop-down list. The New Call dialog box appears (see Figure 13.5).

FIGURE 13.5   You can quickly make a call to a contact using the Autodialer.

2. Click the Start Call button to allow Outlook to dial the contact's phone number using your modem.

3. The Call Status dialog box appears. Pick up your phone and click the Talk button in the Call Status dialog box. This will engage the phone and you can speak to your contact when they answer the call.

VIEWING A MAP OF A CONTACT'S ADDRESS

A very useful feature offered by Outlook is the ability to view an area Map based on the address of a particular contact. This can be incredibly useful when you aren't sure where a particular contact is located.

To view a map of a contact's address, double-click on the contact in the Contacts list. The Contact's record will open in the Contact dialog box.

Click the Display Map of Address button on the Contact toolbar. Microsoft Internet Explorer will open to the Microsoft Expedia Web site and display a map based on the contact's address as shown in Figure 13.6.

You can zoom in and out on the map and you can print a hard copy. When you are done viewing the map, close the Internet Explorer window and you will be returned to the Contact dialog box and Outlook. For more information on using Outlook with Web tools like Internet Explorer see Lesson 26, "Outlook 2000 and the Internet."

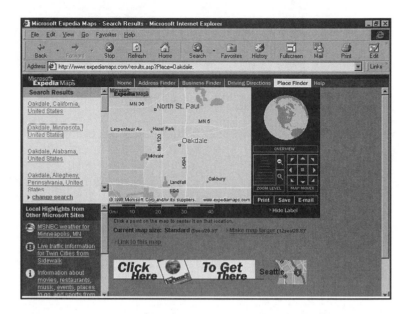

FIGURE 13.6   You can view a map of a Contact's address.

In this lesson, you learned to create a Contacts list, view the list, and send mail to someone on your Contacts list. You also learned to view a map of a contact's address. In the next lesson, you learn to plan and schedule a meeting using Outlook.

Lesson 14

Planning a Meeting

In this lesson you learn to schedule a meeting, enter attendees for a planned meeting, set the meeting date and time, and invite others to the meeting.

Scheduling a Meeting

Outlook enables you to plan the time and date of a meeting, identify the subject and location of the meeting, invite others to attend the meeting, and identify resources that will be needed for the meeting. You use the Calendar folder to plan and schedule meetings.

 Meeting In Outlook, a meeting is an appointment to which you invite others.

Attendees The people who will be attending your meeting.

Resources Any equipment you use in your meeting, such as a computer, a slide projector, or even the room itself.

To plan a meeting, follow these steps:

1. Click the Calendar folder icon on the Outlook bar, and then choose Actions, Plan a Meeting. The Plan a Meeting dialog box appears (see Figure 14.1).

Green bar is starting time

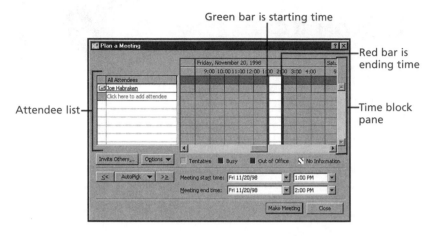

FIGURE **14.1**   Choose the date and time of your meeting as well as the attendees.

2. To enter the names of the attendees, click in the All Attendees list where it says **Click Here to Add Attendee**. Type a name in the box and then press Enter. Continue adding new names as necessary. A better way to invite attendees to your meeting is to click the Invite Others button and choose the attendees from your Personal Address Book or the Outlook Address Book. This makes it easier to email invitations to those whom you want to attend.

3. To set a date for the meeting, open the Meeting Start Time drop-down list and either select the date from the calendar or type the date in the text box. The ending date (in the Meeting End Time drop-down list) automatically shows the same date you set in the Meeting Start Time date box; you can change the End Time date if you want.

4. To set a start time for the meeting, do one of the following:

- Open the Meeting Start Time drop-down list and select the time.

- Type a time in the text box.

- Drag the green bar in the time block pane of the dialog box to set the start time.

5. To set an end time for the meeting, do one of the following:

   • Open the Meeting End Time drop-down list, and select the end time.

   • Type a time in the text box.

   • Drag the red bar in the time block pane of the dialog box to change the ending time of the meeting.

After you select the date and time for the meeting, the time grid to the right of each attendee's name displays other appointments they have scheduled on that day. The times blocked out in each attendee's grid are based on entries in their Outlook Calendar. Outlook can check your corporate network and determine attendee availability by using their calendars. If there is a conflict between your meeting time and an attendee's availability, you can adjust the time of your meeting and avoid scheduling conflicts.

6. When you finish planning the meeting, click the Make Meeting button. The Meeting window appears from which you can refine the meeting details, as described in the next section.

 Use AutoPick to Shift Meeting Time Frame   Click the AutoPick decrease or increase buttons to shift the meeting time (including the beginning and ending) to a half hour earlier or later, respectively. Each time you click AutoPick, the meeting shifts another half hour.

WORKING OUT MEETING DETAILS

After you plan a meeting, Outlook enables you to send invitations, identify the subject of the meeting, and specify the meeting's location. You enter these details in the Meeting dialog box.

When you schedule a meeting, you finish by clicking the Make Meeting button in the Plan a Meeting dialog box. Outlook displays the Meeting dialog box with the Appointment tab in front (see Figure 14.2).

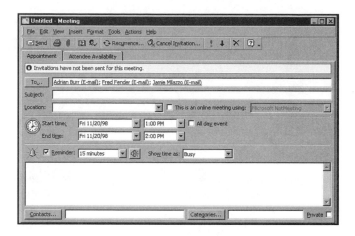

FIGURE 14.2 Specify the details related to the meeting in the Appointment tab of the Meeting dialog box.

Follow these steps to specify details for a meeting you've already scheduled:

1. If you did not list the attendees in the Plan a Meeting dialog box, either click in the To text box and enter the names of the people you want to attend the meeting, or click the To button to select the attendees from an Address Book or Contacts list.

2. In the Subject text box, enter a subject for the meeting.

3. In the Location text box, enter a location for the meeting.

4. (Optional) You can change the starting and ending dates and times in the Appointment tab. You also can choose the Attendee Availability tab to view the meeting in a format similar to that of the Plan a Meeting dialog box; make any changes to attendees, time, dates, and so on in the Attendee Availability tab.

5. (Optional) Select the Reminder check box and enter a time for Outlook to sound an alarm to remind you of the meeting.

6. (Optional) Enter any special text you want to send to the attendees in the text box provided.

About the Online Meeting Check Box   If you plan to hold your meeting online using Microsoft NetMeeting, select the This Is an Online Meeting check box on the Appointment tab of the Meeting dialog box. Scheduling an online meeting is no different than scheduling a face-to-face meeting; you follow the same steps outlined in this lesson. An online meeting, however, requires that you specify a Directory Server (this will appear as a drop-down box when you select the online meeting check box) that will be used to connect the participants. Using NetMeeting is covered in Lesson 26, "Outlook 2000 and the Internet."

7. When you're ready to send the invitations to the meeting, click the Send button. Close the Meeting window by choosing File, Close.

When you send an invitation, you're sending an email that requests the presence of the recipient at the meeting. The recipient can reply to your message, save your message, and forward or delete the message, just as he can with any other email message. If you want the recipient to reply, choose Appointment, Request Responses, and the recipient will be prompted to reply to your invitation.

 An Invitation Mistake   To cancel an invitation after you've sent it, choose Appointment, Cancel Invitation.

INVITING OTHERS TO THE MEETING

If you need to add names to your attendees list—either while you're planning the meeting or at some later date—you can use your Personal Address Book, the Outlook Address Book, or your Contacts list to find the names of the people you want to invite. Additionally, you can choose whether to make the meeting required or optional for each person you invite.

To invite others to the meeting, follow these steps:

1. In either the Plan a Meeting dialog box or the Attendee Availability tab, click the Invite Others button. The Select Attendees and Resources dialog box appears, as shown in Figure 14.3.

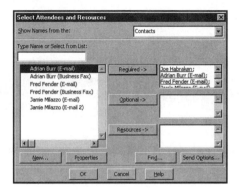

FIGURE 14.3   Use the address books to specify attendees to invite to your meeting.

2. Open the Show Names From The drop-down list and choose either Personal Address Book or Contacts.

3. To add a new name to a list, click the New button and then enter the name, email address, phone numbers, and other pertinent information.

4. Select any name in the list on the left side of the dialog box and click the Required or Optional button to specify attendance requirements.

 Reserve Resources   Click the New button to add resources to the list; then notify the person who is in charge of those resources of your meeting.

5. Click OK to close the dialog box and add any attendees to your list.

EDITING A MEETING

You can edit the details about a meeting, invite additional people, or change the date and time of the meeting at any time by opening the Meeting dialog box.

To open the Meeting dialog box and edit the meeting, follow these steps:

1. In the Calendar folder, choose the meeting date in the monthly calendar pane. The date appears in the schedule pane, and the meeting is blocked out for the time period you specified, as shown in Figure 14.4.

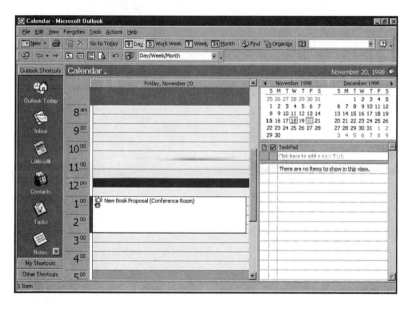

FIGURE 14.4   Select the meeting you want to edit from within the Calendar.

2. Double-click the meeting block to display the Meeting dialog box. You can edit anything in the Appointment or Meeting Planner tabs.

Any Responses? Choose the Show Attendee Status option in the Attendee Availability tab of the Meeting dialog box to see if the people you invited to the meeting have responded to your invitation.

3. When you're done, choose File, Close to close the Meeting dialog box. If you've made changes to the meeting specifics, you should also send a message to your attendees to notify them of the change.

In this lesson you learned to schedule a meeting, enter attendees for a planned meeting, set the meeting time, and invite others to the meeting. In the next lesson you learn to use the Calendar.

LESSON 15
USING THE
CALENDAR

In this lesson you learn to navigate the Calendar, as well as create and save appointments.

NAVIGATING THE CALENDAR

You can use Outlook's Calendar to schedule appointments and create a to-do list; if necessary, Outlook can also remind you of appointments and daily or weekly tasks. You can schedule appointments, move appointments, cancel appointments, and so on. The Calendar makes it easy to identify the days on which you have appointments.

To open the Outlook Calendar, either click the Calendar icon in the Outlook bar or select the Calendar folder from the Folder list. Figure 15.1 shows the Calendar in Outlook.

Outlook provides multiple ways for you to move around in the Calendar and view specific dates:

- Scroll through the Appointment pane to view the time of an appointment.

- In the monthly calendar pane, click the left and right arrows, which are next to the names of the months. They enable you to go backward and forward one month at a time.

Changing Calendar Views You can change to different views of the Calendar by clicking the current view drop-down arrow on the Advanced toolbar. Views including Active Appointments, Recurring Appointments, and By Category are available.

Today's date

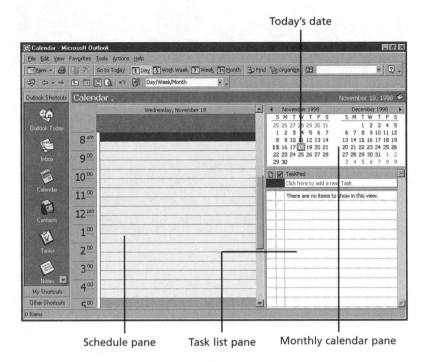

Schedule pane   Task list pane   Monthly calendar pane

FIGURE 15.1   You can view all appointments and tasks at a glance.

- In the monthly calendar pane, click a date to display that date in the schedule pane.

- To switch to a different month in the schedule pane, click the current month in the monthly calendar pane and select the name of the month from the shortcut list.

- To view a week or selected days in the schedule pane, select the days in the monthly calendar pane.

- To add a task to the Task list, click where you see **Click Here to Add a New Task**.

- Use the scrollbars for the Task list pane to view additional tasks, if necessary.

Change the Date Quickly   To quickly go to today's date or to a specific date without searching through the monthly calendar pane, right-click in the schedule pane and choose either Go To Today or Go To Date.

CREATING AN APPOINTMENT

You can create an appointment on any day well past the year 2000 using the Outlook Calendar. When you create an appointment, you can add the subject, location, starting time, category, and even an alarm to remind you ahead of time.

Follow these steps to create an appointment:

1. In the monthly calendar pane, select the month and the date for which you want to create an appointment.

2. In the schedule pane, double-click next to the time at which the appointment is scheduled to begin. The Untitled - Appointment dialog box appears, with the Appointment tab displayed (see Figure 15.2).

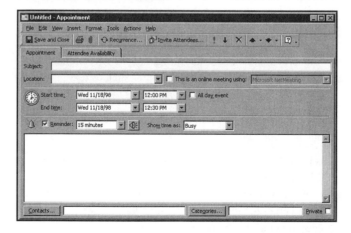

FIGURE 15.2   Enter all the details you need when scheduling an appointment.

3. Enter the subject of the appointment in the Subject text box. (You can use a person's name, a topic, or other information.)

4. In the Location text box, enter the meeting place or other text that will help you identify the meeting when you see it in your calendar.

5. Either enter dates and times in the Start Time and End Time boxes or click the drop-down arrows and select the dates and times.

 Autodate It! You can use Outlook's Autodate feature: Enter a text phrase such as "next Friday" or "noon" in the date box and then press Enter. Outlook figures out the date for you and places it in the date box.

6. Select the Reminder check box and enter the amount of time before the appointment that you want to be notified. If you want to set an audio alarm, click the alarm bell button and select a specific sound for Outlook to play as your reminder.

7. From the Show Time As drop-down list, choose how you want to display the scheduled time on your calendar.

8. In the large text box near the bottom of the Appointment tab, enter any text that you want to include (such as text to identify the appointment, reminders for materials to take, and so on).

9. Click the Categories button and assign a category (or categories) to the appointment.

10. Click the Save and Close button to return to the calendar.

The Attendee Availability tab enables you to schedule a meeting with coworkers and enter the meeting on your Calendar. See Lesson 14, "Planning a Meeting," for more information.

SCHEDULING A RECURRING APPOINTMENT

Suppose you have an appointment that comes around every week or month, or that otherwise occurs on a regular basis. Instead of scheduling every individual occurrence of the appointment, you can schedule that appointment in your calendar as a recurring appointment.

To schedule a recurring appointment, follow these steps:

1. In the Calendar folder, choose the Actions menu, then New Recurring Appointment. The Appointment dialog box appears, and then the Appointment Recurrence dialog box appears on top of the Appointment dialog box (as shown in Figure 15.3).

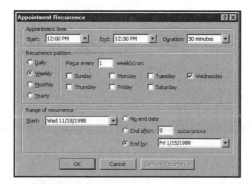

FIGURE 15.3   Schedule a recurring appointment once and Outlook fills in the appointment for you throughout the Calendar.

2. In the Appointment Time area, enter the Start, End, and Duration times for the appointment.

3. In the Recurrence Pattern area, indicate the frequency of the appointment: Daily, Weekly, Monthly, or Yearly. After you select one of these options, the rest of the Recurrence Pattern area changes.

4. Enter the day and month, as well as any other options that are specific to your selection in Step 3, in the Recurrence Pattern area.

5. In the Range of Recurrence area, enter appropriate time limits according to these guidelines:

- **Start**   Choose the date on which the recurring appointments will begin.

- **No End Date**   Choose this option if the recurring appointments are not on a limited schedule.

- **End After**   Choose this option and enter the number of appointments if there is a specific limit to the recurring appointments.

- **End By**   Choose this option and enter an ending date to limit the number of recurring appointments.

6. Click OK to close the Appointment Recurrence dialog box. The Appointment dialog box appears.

7. Fill in the Appointment dialog box as described previously in this lesson. When you finish, click the Save and Close button to return to the Calendar. The recurring appointment appears in your calendar on the specified date and time. A recurring appointment contains a double-arrow icon to indicate that it is recurring.

 Recurring Meetings   You can schedule a recurring meeting by clicking the Actions menu and then selecting New Recurring Meeting. The Appointment dialog box and Recurrence dialog box will both be opened by this Calendar menu selection. Meetings are covered in Lesson 14.

PLANNING EVENTS

In the Outlook Calendar, an *event* is any activity that lasts at least 24 hours, such as a trade show or a conference. You can plan an event in the Calendar program and block off larger time slots than you would for normal appointments. In addition, you can schedule recurring events.

To schedule an event, choose Actions, New All Day Event. The Event dialog box appears (see Figure 15.4). It looks very much like the New Appointment dialog box. Fill in the Subject, Location, Start Time, and End Time text boxes. Make sure the All Day Event check box is selected (which is the only difference between an Event and an Appointment). Click the Save and Close button to return to the Outlook Calendar. The appointment appears in gray at the beginning of the day for which you scheduled the event.

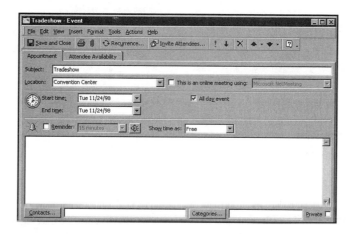

FIGURE **15.4**   You can block out an entire day on the Calendar by scheduling an All Day Event.

To schedule a recurring event, open a New All Day Event window and fill in the information as described earlier. To make the event recurring, click the Recurrence button in the Event window. The Event Recurrence dialog box opens; fill in the appropriate information and click OK. Complete the information in the Event window and then click the Save and Close button.

To edit an event or a recurring event, double-click the event in your Calendar. As with a mail message or appointment, Outlook opens the event window so you can change times, dates, or other event details.

In this lesson you learned to navigate the Calendar, as well as how to create and save appointments. In the next lesson you learn to create a task list.

LESSON 16

CREATING A
TASK LIST

In this lesson you learn to enter a task and record statistics about the task.

ENTERING A TASK

You can use the Tasks folder to create and manage your task list. You can list due dates, status, and priorities, and even set reminder alarms so you don't forget to perform certain tasks. To enter the Tasks folder, click the Task shortcut in the Outlook bar.

 Task List A task list is a list of things you must do to complete your work, such as plan for a meeting, arrange an event, and so on. Various tasks might include making a phone call, writing a letter, printing a spreadsheet, or making airline reservations.

To enter a task, follow these steps:

1. In the Tasks folder, choose Actions, New Task or click the New Task button on the toolbar. The Untitled - Task dialog box appears (see Figure 16.1).

 Double-Click to Start New Task Double-click in any space on the Task window and a new task will open. You can also use this technique with other Outlook items such as appointments and contacts when you are in the appropriate folder.

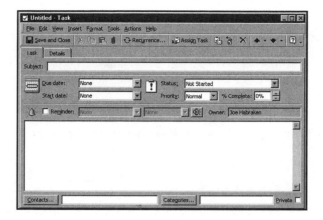

FIGURE 16.1   Enter data such as the subject of the task, due dates, and the task's priority.

2. In the Task tab, enter the subject of the task in the Subject box.

3. Enter a date on which the task should be complete, or click the down arrow to open the Due Date drop-down calendar, and then choose a due date.

4. Enter a start date, or click the down arrow to open the Start Date drop-down calendar, and then choose a starting date.

5. From the Status drop-down list, choose the current status of the project: Not Started, In Progress, Completed, Waiting on Someone Else, or Deferred.

6. In the Priority drop-down list, choose Normal, Low, or High priority.

7. In the % Complete text box, type a percentage or use the spinner arrows to enter one.

8. (Optional) To set an alarm to remind you to start or complete the task, select the Reminder check box and enter a date and a time in the associated text boxes.

9. Enter any comments, descriptions, or other information related to the task in the comments text box.

10. Click the Categories button and choose a category, or enter your own category in the text box.

Access Denied   If you are using Outlook on a corporate network where your folders are kept on the Corporate server, select the Private check box if you don't want others to see information about your task.

11. Click the Save and Close button when you're done.

VIEWING TASKS

As in any Outlook folder, you can change how you view tasks in the list using the current view drop-down list in the Standard toolbar. By default, the Tasks folder displays tasks in Simple List view. Following is a description of the views you can use to display the Tasks folder:

- **Simple List**   Lists the tasks, completed check box, subject, and due date.

- **Detailed List**   Displays the tasks, priority, subject, status, percent completed, and categories.

- **Active Tasks**   Displays the same information as the detailed list but doesn't show any completed tasks.

- **Next Seven Days**   Displays only those tasks you've scheduled for the next seven days, including completed tasks.

- **Overdue Tasks**   Shows a list of tasks that are past due.

- **By Category**   Displays tasks by category; click the button representing the category you want to view.

- **Assignment**   Lists tasks assigned to you by others.

- **By Person Responsible**   Lists tasks grouped by the person who assigned the tasks.

- **Completed Tasks**   Lists only those tasks completed, along with their due dates and completion dates.

- **Task Timeline**   Displays tasks by day, week, or month. Figure 16.2 shows the tasks assigned within one week.

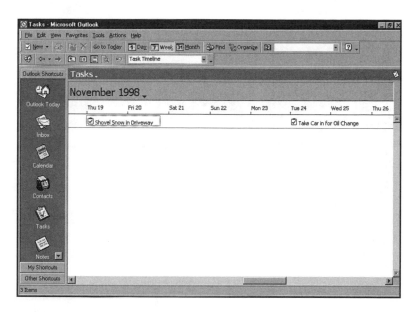

FIGURE 16.2   Double-click a task in Task Timeline view to edit.

    Save What Settings?   Depending on the changes you make to a view, Outlook might display the Save View Settings dialog box asking if you want to save the view settings before you switch to a different view. Generally, you'll want to discard the current view settings and leave everything the way you found it.

MANAGING TASKS

When working with a task list, you can add and delete tasks, mark tasks as completed, and arrange the tasks within the list. You also can perform any of these procedures in most of the task views described in the preceding section. For information about printing a task list, see Lesson 19, "Printing in Outlook."

Figure 16.3 shows the Tasks folder, the following list describes how to manage certain tasks in the list.

Completed task   Click here to sort by due date

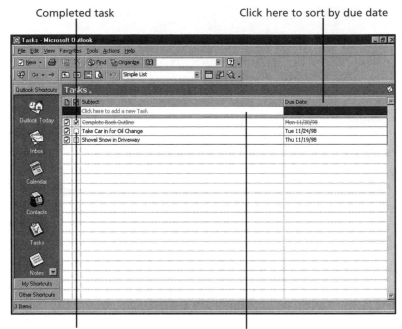

Check here to complete a task   Quickly add new task here

FIGURE 16.3   Add, delete, and sort the tasks in your list.

- To quickly add a task, click the top row of the task list where it says **Click Here to Add a New Task** and enter the subject and date.

- To edit a task, double-click the task in the list. The task dialog box appears.

- To mark a task as completed, either click the check box in the second column or right-click the task and choose Mark Complete from the shortcut menu. Outlook places a line through the task.

- To delete a task, right-click the task and choose Delete from the shortcut menu.

- To assign a task to someone else, right-click the task and choose Assign Task from the shortcut menu. Fill in the name of the person to whom you want to assign the task, and click the Send button to email him or her the task request.

• To assign a new task to someone else, choose Tasks, New Task Request. Create the task as you normally would, but send the task as an email by clicking the Send button.

 Get Rid of the Default Task   If you don't want to leave the Start Up Microsoft Outlook task on your list, right-click the task and choose Delete.

RECORDING STATISTICS ABOUT A TASK

You can record statistics about a task, such as time spent completing the task, billable time, contacts, and so on, for your own records or for reference when sharing tasks with your co-workers. This feature is particularly helpful when you assign tasks to others; you can keep track of assigned tasks and find out when they're completed.

To enter statistics about a task, open any task in the task list and click the Details tab. Figure 16.4 shows a completed Details tab for a sample task.

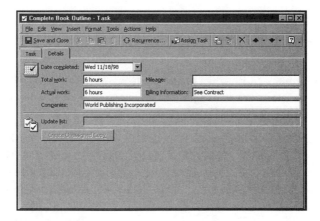

FIGURE **16.4**   Fill in the status of the task so you can share it with others and keep personal records.

Export Task Lists You can export task lists and other Outlook information to a variety of applications, such as Microsoft Excel. Click File, Import and Export. A wizard will walk you through the steps so that you can place the appropriate task information in the cells of a spreadsheet or in a document in a word processor.

The following list describes the text boxes in the Details tab as well as the types of information you can enter:

- **Date Completed** Enter the date the task was completed, or click the arrow to display the calendar and choose the date.

- **Total Work** Enter the amount of time you expect the task to take. When you complete the job, Outlook calculates the actual time spent and enters it in this text box.

- **Actual Work** Enter the amount of time it actually took to complete the job.

- **Mileage** Enter the number of miles you traveled to complete the task.

- **Billing Information** Enter any specific billing information, such as hours billed, resources used, charges for equipment, and so on.

- **Companies** Enter the names of any companies associated with the contacts or with the project in general. Use semicolons to separate multiple names.

- **Update List** Automatically displays the people whose task lists are updated when you've made a change to your task. This is only available in situations where you are on a Corporate network and using the Corporate installation of Outlook where your Task folder is available on the local network.

- **Create Unassigned Copy** Copies the task so it can be reassigned; use the supplied button to send a task to someone other than an original recipient. If the task is not sent to someone else, the button is unavailable.

To track tasks you've assigned to others and to receive status reports, follow these steps:

1. On the Tools menu, click Options; the Options dialog box appears. Click the Other tab, and then click Advanced Options.

2. In the Advanced Options dialog box, click Delegated Tasks. The Delegated Tasks dialog box opens.

3. To automatically track the progress of new tasks you assign to others, select the Keep Updated Copies Of Assigned Tasks On My Task List check box.

4. To automatically receive notification when an assigned task is completed, select the Send Status Reports When Assigned Tasks Are Completed check box.

5. After you've made your selections, click OK in each of the three open dialog boxes to return to the Outlook window.

 Color Your Task List You also can set color options for overdue and completed tasks. Click the Task Options button on the Preferences tab of the Outlook Options dialog box.

In this lesson you learned to enter a task and record statistics about the task. In the next lesson you learn to use the Journal.

LESSON 17
USING THE JOURNAL

In this lesson you learn to create journal entries manually and automatically and to change views in the Journal.

CREATING A JOURNAL ENTRY

You can create a record of various items and documents to track your work, communications, reports, and so on. In the Journal, you can manually record any activities, items, or tasks you want. You also can automatically record email messages, faxes, meeting requests, meeting responses, task requests, and task responses. Additionally, you can automatically record documents created in the other Office applications such as Access, Excel, Office Binder, PowerPoint, and Word.

The Journal is especially useful for recording phone calls to and from contacts. This enables you to not only record the call as a Journal entry, but also to time the conversation and record its duration. For information about calling a contact, see Lesson 13, "Creating a Contacts List."

Journal A folder within Outlook that you can use to record interactions, phone calls, message responses, and other activities important to your work.

Item An article or object in Outlook, such as a task, appointment, or contact.

You can automatically or manually record items in your journal. You can, for example, choose to automatically record your email messages, meeting requests, task responses, and so on.

The first time you click the Journal folder to open it (in the Folder list or the Outlook bar), a message appears asking if you want to turn the Journal feature on. Click Yes. The Journal Options dialog box appears. In this dialog box you can specify what types of events you want automatically recorded in the Journal. Check boxes are provided to include email messages, meeting requests, and other events that are received from people in your Contacts folder (click the check box for the specific contact). You also can open files in Access, Excel, PowerPoint, and Word by checking the appropriate check box.

When you have completed your selections, click OK. The Journal opens and automatically records the items you chose in the Journal Options dialog box. (For more information on the Journal Options dialog box, see "Automatically Recording Entries," later in this lesson.)

You also can record items in the Journal manually. For example, you might add an email message to the Journal that is not normally recorded (because you didn't select messages from that particular contact as something you want automatically recorded in the Journal).

RECORDING AN ENTRY MANUALLY

To create a journal entry manually, follow these steps:

1. In the Inbox folder (or any other folder in Outlook), select the item you want to record in the Journal and drag it onto the Journal folder in the Outlook bar. The Journal Entry dialog box appears (see Figure 17.1).

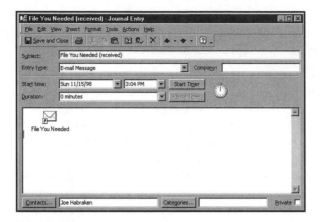

Figure 17.1 Drag any item from a folder onto the journal icon in the Outlook bar to add the item to the Journal.

2. The information in the Subject, Entry Type, Contact, and Company boxes (as well as other information from the selected item) is automatically entered for you. However, you can change any of the statistics you want by entering new information in the text boxes. The following is a list of the text boxes available in the Journal Entry dialog box:

- **Subject**   Displays the title or name of the item.

- **Entry Type**   Describes the item based on its point of origin, such as a Word document, Meeting or Appointment, and so on.

- **Contact**   Lists the name(s) of any attendees, contacts, or other people involved with the selected item.

- **Company**   Lists the company or companies associated with the contacts.

- **Start Time**   Displays the date and time of the meeting, appointment, or other item.

- **Start Timer**   Records the time that passes until you click the Pause Timer button.

- **Pause Timer**   Stops the timer.

- **Duration**   Displays the amount of time taken to complete the item.

- **Text Box**   Displays a shortcut to the item itself, such as the Calendar appointment, Contact, or Message that you originally dragged onto the Journal folder. You can open the item by double-clicking on the shortcut icon.

- **Categories**   Enter or select a category in which to place the item.

3. Click Save and Close to complete the Journal entry.

Time Your Calls   When making phone calls or meeting with clients, create a journal entry to record the event, and use the Start Timer and Pause Timer buttons to record billable time. When you start the Timer, notice that the duration of the Journal entry is recorded in the Duration box. This is updated each minute. When you complete the Journal entry the total time is reflected in the Duration box.

If you want to create a new journal entry, but you don't have a contact, task, email, or other item that you want to use to create the entry, you can manually record a journal entry by following these steps:

1. Change to the Journal folder.

2. Choose Actions, New Journal Entry or click the New Journal Entry button on the Standard or Advanced toolbar. The Journal Entry dialog box appears.

3. Enter the subject, entry type, contact, time, and any other information you want to record.

4. When you finish, click the Save and Close button.

AUTOMATICALLY RECORDING ENTRIES

You can set options to automatically record items and their related contacts and/or statistics about Microsoft Office documents you create. Suppose, for example, that you want to keep a record of all memos you send to your boss. You can record them in your journal. When you first open the Journal, you have the option of setting automatic entries in the Journal Options dialog box. You also can change your settings or add additional items to the automatically recorded list.

To set the options to automatically record journal entries, follow these steps:

1. In the Journal folder, choose Tools, Options. The Options dialog box appears. Click the Preferences tab if necessary, then click the Journal Options button. The Journal Options dialog box appears, as shown in Figure 17.2.

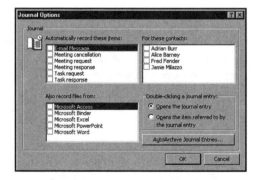

FIGURE 17.2   The Journal Options dialog box is where you set the options for automatically recording items in your Journal.

2. In the Automatically Record These Items list, check those items you want Outlook to automatically record in your journal. (The items recorded correspond with the people selected in the list of contacts in step 3.)

3. In the For These Contacts list, check any contacts you want automatically recorded in the Journal. Outlook records any items checked in step 2 that apply to the selected contacts.

4. In the Also Record Files From list, check the applications for which you want to record journal entries. Outlook records the date and time you create or modify files in the selected program.

You also can choose to have your Journal entries AutoArchived. Click the AutoArchive Journal Entries button and then choose a folder on your computer where you would like to have the Journal Archive file stored. Click OK to complete the process. For more information about the AutoArchive feature, see Lesson 23, "Archiving Items."

Automatic and Easy   When you're creating a new contact in Outlook, you can set items to be automatically recorded in the Journal by choosing the Journal tab in the Contact dialog box and checking the Automatically Record Journal Entries for This Contact check box.

VIEWING JOURNAL ENTRIES

By default, the Journal folder displays information in Task Timeline view and By Type, as shown in Figure 17.3. However, you can display the entries in various views, as described in the following list. To select a particular view, click the current view drop-down button on the Advanced toolbar.

Save Settings?   As in other views, Outlook might display the Save View Settings dialog box to ask if you want to save the view settings before you switch to a different view. You're probably getting used to this dialog box by now.

Current view   Double-click to view entries

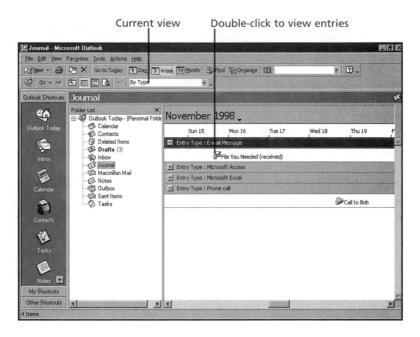

FIGURE 17.3   View the journal entries by type.

- **By Type**   In Task Timeline view, this option groups journal entries by type, such as email messages, meetings, Word documents, and so on. Double-click a type to display its contents, and then position the mouse pointer over an entry to view its contents or name.

Using Journal Options?   When you switch to the Journal in By Type view, a Journal Options dialog box appears. This dialog box enables you to specify which email messages will be recorded in the Journal based on the contact who sent them. You can also use the Journal to record when you use certain applications. For instance, if you want a journal entry placed in the journal when you use Microsoft Word or Microsoft Access, you can set this option in the Options dialog box.

- **By Contact**   In Task Timeline view, this displays the name of each contact that you selected in the Options dialog box. Double-click any contact's name to view recorded entries.

- **By Category**   If you've assigned categories to your journal entries and other items, you can display your journal entries by category in Task Timeline view.

- **Entry List**   Displays entries in a table with columns labeled Entry Type, Subject, Start, Duration, Contact, and Categories.

- **Last Seven Days**   Displays entries in an entry list, but includes only those entries dated within the last seven days.

- **Phone Calls**   Lists all entries that are phone calls.

Sort Journal Entries   You can click the heading bar—Subject, Start, or Duration—in any entry list view to sort the items in that column in ascending or descending order.

In this lesson you learned to create journal entries manually and automatically and to change views in the Journal. In the next lesson you learn to create notes.

LESSON 18

USING OUTLOOK NOTES

In this lesson you learn to create, sort, and view notes.

CREATING NOTES

If you've ever used a paper sticky note to remind yourself of tasks, ideas, or other brief annotations, Outlook's Notes are for you. Notes are similar to paper sticky notes. You can use Notes to write down reminders, names, phone numbers, directions, or anything else you need to remember. In Outlook, all notes are kept in the Notes folder. You'll have to remember to look at the folder so you can view your notes.

 The Long and Short of It Notes don't have to be brief. You can enter pages and pages of text if you want. As you type, the page scrolls for you; use the arrow keys and the Page Up/Page Down keys to move through the note text. Keep in mind, however, that the purpose of the note is to be a quick reminder, or to hold information that you will eventually transfer to one of the other Outlook items, such as an appointment or task.

To create a note, click the Notes folder on the Outlook bar and then follow these steps:

1. In the Notes folder, either choose Actions, New Note or click the
   New Note button on the Standard or Advanced toolbar. A note
   appears, ready for you to type your text.

2. Enter the text for your note (see Figure 18.1).

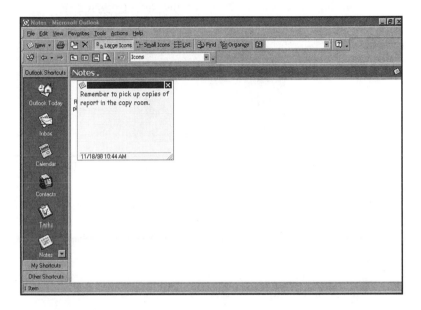

FIGURE 18.1   A note automatically includes the date and time it
was created.

3. When you finish, click the Close (X) button to close the note.
   You can reopen a note and enter more text or edit text as necessary.

If you press Enter after typing text in the note, you create a line break and
you create a title, of sorts, at the same time. Only the text before the hard
return displays when the note is closed. If you do not add a hard return,
but enter the note text so that it automatically wraps from line to line, the
entire note text appears below the note in Icons view.

SETTING NOTE OPTIONS

You can change the default color and size of your notes. You also can change the default font used for your notes. To set note options, follow these steps:

1. In the Notes folder (or any of the Outlook folders), choose Tools, Options. The Options dialog box appears. On the Preferences tab, click Note Options; the Notes Options dialog box appears (see Figure 18.2).

FIGURE **18.2** Customize your notes in the Notes Options dialog box.

2. In the Color drop-down list, you can change the color of your notes to Yellow, Blue, Green, Pink, or White. The default is Yellow.

3. In the Size drop-down list choose Small, Medium, or Large for the size of the notes. The default is Medium.

4. To change the font, click the Font button. The Font dialog box appears. Change the font, font style, size, color, and other options, and then click OK.

MANAGING INDIVIDUAL NOTES

To open an existing note, double-click it in the Notes folder. You can edit the text in an open note as you would edit any text. To move a note, drag its title bar. You can delete, forward, or print notes; you can change the color of individual notes; and you can specify categories for your notes.

You also can drag the notes to the Windows desktop and arrange them there.

Click an open note's Control button to display a menu with the following options:

- **New Note**   Creates a new note but leaves the first note open.

- **Save As.**   Enables you to save the note and its contents.

- **Delete**   Deletes a note and its contents. (You also can delete a note by selecting it in the Notes list and pressing Delete.)

- **Forward**   Enables you to send the note as an attachment in an email message.

- **Cut, Copy, Paste**   Enables you to select text from the note and cut or copy it to the Clipboard. The Paste command enables you to paste items on the Clipboard at the insertion point in the note.

- **Color**   Choose another color for the individual note.

- **Categories**   Enter or choose a category.

- **Print**   Print the contents of the note.

- **Close**   Closes the note. (You also can click the Close (X) button in the note's title bar.) A closed note appears in the Notes folder.

VIEWING NOTES

The Notes folder provides various views for organizing and viewing your notes. You also can sort notes in any entry list view by right-clicking the heading bar—Subject, Created, Categories, and so on—and selecting the sort method.

The default view is Icons, but you can change the view using the current view drop-down list in the Standard toolbar. Figure 18.3 shows the Notes folder in the default view.

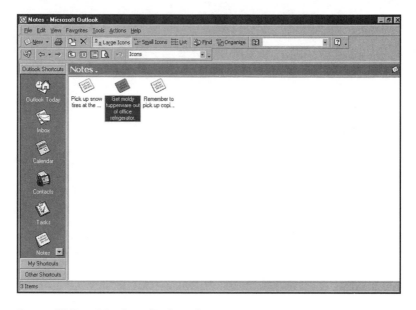

FIGURE 18.3   This view displays the notes in Icons view.

You can choose to display your Notes folder in any of the following views:

- **Icons**   Displays the notes as note icons with the message (or a portion of the message) displayed below the icon.

- **Notes List**   Displays the notes in a list, showing the title and note contents in the Subject column, the creation date and time, and the categories.

- **Last Seven Days**   Displays all notes written in the last seven days, by subject, creation date, and categories.

- **By Category**   Displays the categories; double-click a category to show its contents.

- **By Color**   Displays notes by their color. Double-click a color to display the notes.

In this lesson you learned to create, sort, and view notes. In the next lesson you learn to print in Outlook.

LESSON 19

PRINTING IN OUTLOOK

In this lesson you learn to print items in Outlook, change the page setup, preview an item before printing it, and change printer properties.

CHOOSING PAGE SETUP

In Outlook, before you print, you choose the print style you want to use. Each folder—Inbox, Calendar, Contacts, and so on—offers various print styles, and each style displays the data on the page in a different way.

Page In Outlook, this is the area of the paper that will actually be printed on. You can, for example, print two or four pages on a single sheet of paper.

Print Style The combination of paper and page settings that control printed output.

You can choose from Outlook's built-in print styles, modify the default print styles, or create your own print styles. The following lists show the default print styles available for each folder. To access the print styles for a particular item, select File, Print. The Inbox, Contacts, and Tasks use the Table style and the Memo style; the Journal and Notes use only the Memo style.

- **Table Style**   Displays data in columns and rows on an 8 1/2- by 11-inch sheet, portrait orientation, 1/2-inch margins.

- **Memo Style**   Displays data with a header of information about the message and then straight text on an 8 1/2- by 11-inch sheet, portrait orientation, 1/2-inch margins.

The Calendar folder provides the Memo style, plus the following styles:

- **Daily Style**   Displays one day's appointments on one page on an 8 1/2- by 11-inch sheet, portrait orientation, 1/2-inch margins.

- **Weekly Style**   Displays one week's appointments per page on an 8 1/2- by 11-inch sheet, portrait orientation, 1/2-inch margins.

- **Monthly Style**   Displays one month's appointments per page on an 8 1/2- by 11-inch sheet, landscape orientation, 1/2-inch margins.

- **Tri-Fold Style**   Displays the daily calendar, task list, and weekly calendar on an 8 1/2- by 11-inch sheet, landscape orientation, 1/2-inch margins.

- **Calendar Details Style**   Shows the currently displayed Calendar items and the body text of each item (such as an appointment) in a list format.

The Contacts folder provides the Memo style, plus the following styles:

- **Card Style**   Two columns and headings on an 8 1/2- by 11-inch sheet, portrait orientation, 1/2-inch margins.

- **Small Booklet Style**   One-column pages that print the Contacts in a format similar to mailing labels that place multiple Contacts on a page. This style can be printed in portrait or landscape modes.

- **Medium Booklet Style**   One column that equals 1/4 of a sheet of paper so that four pages are on one 8 1/2- by 11-inch sheet of paper, portrait orientation with 1/2-inch margins.

- **Phone Directory Style**   One column, 8 1/2- by 11-inch sheet of paper, portrait orientation with 1/2-inch margins.

Page Setup Only Matters in Printing   No matter how you set up your pages, it will not affect your view of tasks, calendars, or other Outlook items onscreen. Page setup only applies to a print job.

You can view, modify, and create new page setups in Outlook. To view or edit a page setup, follow these steps:

1. Change to the folder for which you're setting the page.

2. Choose File, then point at Page Setup. A secondary menu appears that lists the available print types.

3. Select the print type you want to view or edit, and the Page Setup dialog box appears (see Figure 19.1).

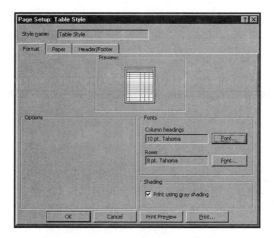

FIGURE **19.1**   Customize the print style to suit yourself.

4. Click the Format tab to view or edit the page type, to choose options (in some cases), and to change fonts.

5. Click the Paper tab to view or edit paper size, page size, margins, and orientation.

6. Click the Header/Footer tab to view or edit headers and footers
for your pages.

PREVIEWING BEFORE PRINTING

You can choose to preview an item before printing it so you're sure it
looks the way you want it to look. If you do not like the way an item
looks in preview, you can change the page setup.

Before you display an item in Print Preview, you must change to the
folder containing the item you want to print. Then you can choose to preview the item in any of the following ways:

- Click the Print Preview button in the Page Setup dialog box.

- Choose File, Print Preview.

- Click the Print Preview button on the Advanced toolbar.

- Click the Preview button in the Print dialog box.

Figure 19.2 shows a calendar and task list in Print Preview. You can
change the page setup by clicking the Page Setup button; the Page Setup
dialog box appears. Click the Print button to send the job to the printer.
Click the Close button to exit Print Preview and return to the Outlook
folder.

Enlarge the View   When the mouse pointer looks like
a magnifying glass with a plus sign in it, you can click
to enlarge the page. When the mouse pointer looks
like a magnifying glass with a minus sign in it, you can
click to reduce the view again.

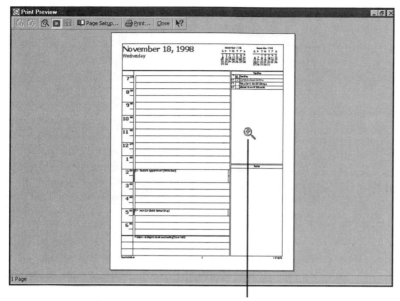

Mouse pointer changes to a magnifying glass

FIGURE 19.2   Preview an item before printing it.

PRINTING ITEMS

After you choose the print style and preview an item to make sure it's what you want, you can print the item. You can indicate the number of copies you want to print, select a printer, change the print style or page setup, and set a print range.

When you're ready to print an item, follow these steps:

1. Choose File, Print or click the Print button on the Standard toolbar. The Print dialog box appears, as shown in Figure 19.3.

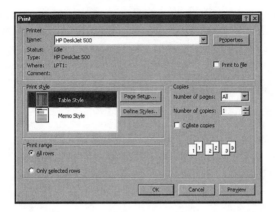

FIGURE 19.3   Set the printing options before printing an item.

2. In the Printer area of the dialog box, choose a different printer from the Name drop-down list if necessary.

3. In the Print Style area, choose a print style from the list. You also can edit the page setup (with the Page Setup button) or edit or create a new style (with the Define Styles button).

4. In the Copies area, choose All, Even, or Odd in the Number of Pages drop-down list. Enter the number of copies you want to print in the Number of Copies drop-down list. Click the Collate Copies check box if you want Outlook to automatically assemble multiple copies.

5. Set the print range with the options in that area. (The Print Range options vary depending on the type of item you're printing.)

6. Click OK to print the item.

Printing Mailing Labels and Envelopes   A really handy Outlook feature is the ability to print mailing labels and envelopes from your Contacts list. To take advantage of this feature, you need to have Word 2000 installed on your computer. Creating form letters, mailing labels, or envelopes is called a *mail merge*. Basically, you create some type of main document (such as mailing labels, envelopes, and so on) in Word that will hold field codes that relate to the information you keep on each contact, such as name or address. To actually start the merge process, open your Contacts folder and then select Tools, Mail Merge. The Mail Merge Contacts dialog box that appears enables you to specify the contacts for the merge, as well as the Word document that the contact information will be merged into.

SETTING PRINTER PROPERTIES

Whether you're printing to a printer connected directly to your computer or to a printer on the network, you can set printer properties. The properties you set apply to all print jobs you send to the printer until you change the properties again.

Printer Properties   Configurations specific to a printer connected to your computer or to the network. Printer properties include paper orientation, paper source, graphics settings, fonts, and print quality.

Access Denied? If you cannot change the printer properties to a network printer, it's probably because the network administrator has set the printer's configuration and you're not allowed access to the settings. If you need to change printer properties and cannot access the printer's Properties dialog box, talk to your network administrator.

To set printer properties, choose File, Print to open the Print dialog box. In the Printer area, select a printer from the Name drop-down list, and then click the Properties button. The Properties dialog boxes differ depending on the make and model of the printer.

Most likely, you'll be able to set paper size, page orientation, and paper source using options on a Paper tab in the dialog box. In addition, you might see a Graphics tab, in which you can set the resolution, intensity, and graphics mode of your printer. A Fonts tab enables you to set options on TrueType fonts, font cartridges, and so on. You might also find a Device Options tab, in which you can set print quality and other options. For more information about your printer, read the documentation that came with it.

In this lesson you learned to print items in Outlook, change the page setup, preview an item before printing it, and change printer properties. In the next lesson you learn to manage your files and Outlook items.

LESSON 20

SAVING, OPENING, AND FINDING OUTLOOK ITEMS

In this lesson you learn to save items, open items, and find items in Outlook.

SAVING, OPENING, AND USING ITEMS

Generally, when you finish adding a new task, appointment, meeting, contact, or other item, Outlook automatically saves that item for you or you're prompted to save the item yourself. You also can save most items in Outlook for use in other applications by using the Save As command. After you save an item by naming it, you can open that same item and edit, print, or otherwise use the saved file in Windows applications that support the file type. You might save an item—a journal entry or appointment page, for example—so you can refer to it later, edit the original, or keep it as a record.

> **Save As** When you save an item using the File, Save As command, you can designate a drive, directory, and new filename for that item, as well as a file type.

File Type   A file type is the same thing as a file format. When you save a file, you specify a file type that identifies the file as one that can be opened in specific applications. For example, the file extension .DOC identifies a file type that you can open in Word, and the extension .TXT represents a text-only format you can open in nearly any word processor or other application.

Save and Close   This command choice is available when you create new contacts, appointments, and tasks. It saves the current item and closes the item's dialog box, returning you to the currently selected folder, such as the Contacts folder or the Task list.

To save an item, follow these steps:

1. In the folder containing the item you want to save, choose File, Save As. The Save As dialog box appears (see Figure 20.1).

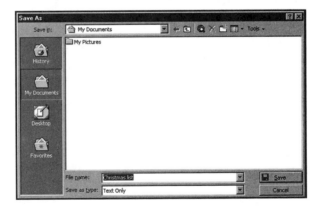

FIGURE 20.1   Save items as files for use in other programs, as copies of the originals, or for later use.

Why Is Save As Dimmed?   When the Save As command is dimmed, you must first select an item—an appointment, meeting, task, note, and so on—before you can save it.

2. From the Save In drop-down list, choose the drive to which you want to save the file. From the folders on that drive, select the one you want to save to (or take advantage of the My Documents or Desktop icons on the left of the dialog box to quickly go to these folders).

3. In the Save As Type drop-down list, choose a file type. You can save the file in Text Only, RTF, Outlook Template, and Message Format.

4. After you choose the type, either enter a name for the item in the File Name text box or accept the default.

5. Click the Save button. Outlook not only enables you to save items in different formats, but it also enables you to open certain file formats and use the files in Outlook. Here is an explanation of several file formats, including how you would save to the particular file type in Outlook and how you would open a file in this format in Outlook.

   Text Only   Saves in ASCII format, which you can use in other applications, such as Word, Notepad, and so on. Save Outlook items in ASCII when you want to send them to someone who does not have Outlook and for whom text-only format will suffice. Any special formatting in the item will be lost when you save in this format. You also can open text-only items in Outlook: Choose File, Open, and then in the Open dialog box, choose Text Only. Select the text file, and click Open. Information in text-only files can be converted into Messages, Tasks, or Contacts.

RTF Text Format   Saves in rich text format. You also can use this format in Word, Outlook, or Lotus Notes, for example. This format enables you to save items for use in other applications and maintains the text formatting such as bold, underline, and so on.

To open an RTF file in Outlook or another Windows application, choose File, Open. In the Open dialog box, choose Rich Text Format (or RTF Text Format) in the Files of Type drop-down list. The saved files appear in the file list. Select the file and click the Open button.

Figure 20.2 shows an email message from Outlook saved as an RTF file and opened in Word. After opening a file, you can format it, cut or copy items to it, insert objects, print, edit, and otherwise manipulate the file. Additionally, you can open the attachment to the email message from within the saved RTF file and read it.

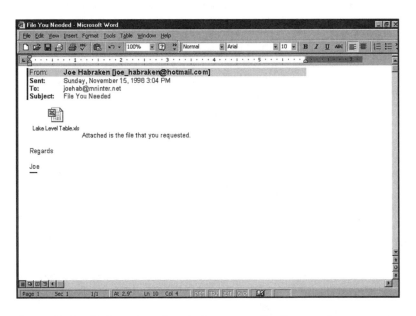

FIGURE 20.2   Exchanging data between applications makes your work easier.

RTF Isn't Listed?   If RTF isn't listed in the application's Files of Type list box, see if Text Only is listed. You also can save Outlook items as Text Only. And if you are using Word as your email editor, you also have the option of saving the mail message in a Word document format.

Outlook Template   Saves as a template (or style sheet) that you can use as a basis for other items. You can open an Outlook template when you are in any of the Outlook folders. Templates supply you with ready-made formatting for your Outlook items.

Message Format   Saves in a format you can use in your email messages. After you save an item as a message text file, you can insert the item into an email message to send. Suppose you saved a contact's information or an especially long note that you want to share with someone else; you can insert the file as an object into a message and send the email as you normally would. The recipient then can open the message and the message file.

To insert a message file into a message, open the message and choose Insert, Object. In the Insert Object dialog box, choose Create from File. Enter the path and filename, and click OK. Figure 20.3 shows a message file in the text of an email.

If you haven't saved the message as a file, you still can insert it as an item into the message you are composing. Choose Insert, Item. The Insert Item dialog box appears. Choose the folder in which the item (such as a mail message) resides using the appropriate folder icon at the top of the dialog box. Select the actual item in the list that appears at the bottom of the dialog box, and then click OK.

Files As Objects   As described in Lesson 9, "Attaching Items to a Message," you can insert any existing file as an object; therefore, you can insert an RTF, text-only, or message file into a Word document, Excel spreadsheet, mail message, or any other Windows document that supports OLE.

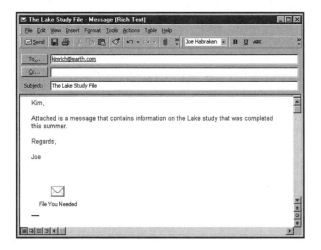

FIGURE 20.3   Open the MSG file by double-clicking its icon.

Use Browse to Find the Object   If you don't remember the location and filename of the object you want to insert in your message, use the Browse button in the Object dialog box to locate the file.

FINDING ITEMS

Outlook provides a Find feature that you can use to locate items in your various Outlook folders. You can search for messages, files, journal entries, notes, tasks, contacts, appointments, and so on, depending on which folder you are currently in (Find can only search through the currently selected folder, such as Inbox or Contacts). When you use the Find feature, it opens in its own pane at the top of the current folder window.

Type in a keyword or phrase, and the Find feature searches all the items in the current folder for your search word or words. When it finds items that match the search phrase, it lists them in the current folder window. Items not matching the search criteria are hidden.

 Criteria   Guidelines you set in the Find dialog box that Outlook uses to find items, such as messages, contacts, or appointments. Included in the criteria you set may be the date an item was created, the title or subject of the item, or specific text within the item.

To find an item in an Outlook folder, follow these steps:

1. Select the folder in which you want to search for the item. Choose Tools, Find or click the Find button on the Standard toolbar. The Find pane appears, as shown in Figure 20.4.

FIGURE 20.4   Use the Find pane to search for items in the current folder.

2. Type your search criteria in the Look For box.

3. When you are ready to run the search, click Find Now.

4. The items that match your search word or phrase appear in the Folder list. (If no matches were found, the message **Did you find it? if not, try** appears followed by two choices: a link to the Advanced find feature and Clear Search.)

5. You can perform a new search by clicking the Clear Search button; enter a new search phrase in the Look For box and then click Find Now. When you have completed your search, you can close the Find pane by clicking its Close button.

USING THE ADVANCED FIND FEATURE

The Find pane includes an Advanced Find button in the upper-right corner. You can use Advanced Find to perform more detailed searches than you can with the Find feature. In the Advanced dialog box, you can set multiple search criteria such as a category, from, sent to, and subject. (When searching for mail messages, additional search criteria exist for each of the other items found in Outlook.)

To use the Advanced Find feature, follow these steps:

1. Open the Advanced Find dialog box by choosing Tools, Advanced Find or clicking the Advanced Find button in the upper-right corner of the Find pane.

2. In the Advanced Find dialog box, set the criteria for your search using the criteria boxes found on the various tabs that appear. For instance, the Message Advanced Find dialog box includes tabs for Messages, More Choices, and Advanced. Each tab provides you with more advanced methods for conducting the search.

3. Set your search conditions on the various tabs. The More Choices tab is the same for each Outlook item and enables you to search for items that have not been read or items that have an attachment.

4. When you've finished setting your criteria, click the Find Now button. A box will open at the bottom of the Advanced dialog box that lists the items that have met the search criteria. To open an item, double-click it.

Figure 20.5 shows the Advanced dialog box with the tabs that are used for searching the Inbox or other message folders. A drop-down list at the top left of the dialog box enables you to change the type of item that you are searching.

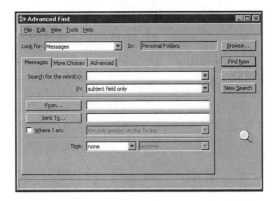

FIGURE 20.5   Set multiple criteria in the Advanced Find dialog box to find specific items.

In this lesson you learned to save items, open items, and find items in Outlook. In the next lesson you learn to integrate items between Outlook folders.

LESSON 21

USING
OUTLOOK
INTEGRATION,
FORMS, AND
TEMPLATES

In this lesson you learn to use various items in Outlook together—to create a task or an appointment from a mail message and to create a document within Outlook, for example. You are also introduced to the Outlook templates.

CREATING A TASK FROM A MAIL MESSAGE

You can use a mail message to easily create a task in Outlook. Instead of printing the message and then opening your Task list to add the information, you can create the task by using drag-and-drop copying. For more information about using the Tasks folder, see Lesson 16, "Creating a Task List."

 You Don't Lose the Message When you use a message to create another item, Outlook copies the message so that the original remains in the Inbox.

To create a task from a mail message, follow these steps:

1. Open the Inbox folder.

2. Click and drag the unopened mail message from the Inbox window to the Tasks icon on the Outlook bar. The Task dialog box opens (see Figure 21.1).

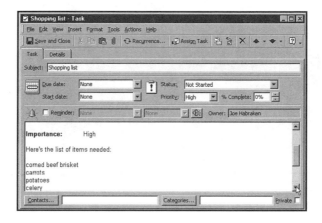

FIGURE 21.1   Create a task from an email message.

3. Change the subject or other data if you want, and then set any options for the task (such as due date, priority, reminders, categories, and so on).

4. Click the Save and Close button, and Outlook adds the task to your list.

CREATING AN APPOINTMENT FROM A MAIL MESSAGE

In addition to creating tasks from messages, you can create an appointment from a mail message. You can set a time and date for the appointment, invite attendees to the appointment, create a meeting, and otherwise set options for the appointment. For more information about creating appointments, see Lesson 15, "Using the Calendar."

To create an appointment from a mail message, follow these steps:

1. Open the Inbox and locate the mail message you want to use.

2. Drag the unopened message from the Inbox window to the Calendar folder on the Outlook bar. The Appointment dialog box opens with some information automatically filled in (see Figure 21.2).

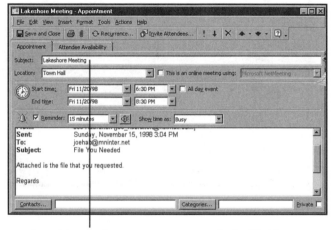

The Subject and Contents are automatically filled in

FIGURE 21.2   Create an appointment using the data in a mail message.

3. Add the location to the appointment and make any desired changes in the Subject, Start Time, or End Time boxes, or in any of the other options.

4. Click the Save and Close button to complete the appointment.

CREATE A NOTE FROM ANY ITEM

Just as you can create tasks and appointments from a mail message, you also can create a note from any item in Outlook. Suppose someone emailed you information about a product or service that you want to add to a report; you can simply create a note with the information on it.

Or suppose you want to call someone at a certain time later in the day. You can create a note from your contact entry so you won't forget.

You can create a note from a mail message, appointment or meeting, contact, task, or journal entry. After you create the note, you can edit the text in the note without affecting the original item.

To create a note from any Outlook item, drag the item to the Notes folder in the Outlook bar. Outlook creates and displays the note, and you can edit the text if you want. For more information about notes, see Lesson 18, "Using Outlook Notes."

USING OUTLOOK FORMS AND TEMPLATES

As you already know, Outlook provides a number of different forms that you can use to create items for your various Outlook folders; there is an Appointment form, a Contact form, a Journal entry form, and so on. In most cases, you choose a particular form when you are in a particular folder; for instance, when you are in the Calendar folder, you open a new Appointment form.

You also can open the various forms that Outlook provides from the File menu, no matter which folder you are working in. This means that you can be in the Inbox folder, and still quickly open a new Appointment form. To open any of Outlook's available forms, select File, point at New, and then select Choose Form. The Choose Form dialog box appears. Select the form you want to use from the list provided in the dialog box, and then click the Open button.

Outlook also includes a number of form templates on which you can base new messages. You can access these templates by using the Choose Form dialog box. The templates offer you alternative layouts and special features such as decorative fonts and graphics to add pizzazz to a new message.

To use an Outlook template for a message, follow these steps:

1. Choose File, New, Choose Form to open the Choose Form dialog box.

2. In the Choose Form dialog box, click the Look In box drop-down arrow and select one of the form libraries listed. The available forms in that library appear in the Choose Form dialog box (see Figure 21.3). The Standard Forms Library contains default forms. Special forms that you have created are found in the Personal Forms Library or in some other location on your computer or on your company's network.

Figure 21.3   Base your new message on a specific form in Outlook.

3. Select the form you want to use and click OK. Outlook displays the message window in which you can create your item.

When you use templates for messages, the person who receives the message must have an email system that can show the special graphics and text formatting options available in the template. If you send messages to people who have a text-only email package, you may want to forgo using the templates. Templates, however, are a good way to dress up your other Outlook items, such as tasks or appointments. (See Lesson 6, "Creating Mail," for more information on using special mail types, such as HTML.)

In this lesson you learned to use various items in Outlook together—to create a task and an appointment from a mail message and to create a document within Outlook. In the next lesson you learn to share data with other Office applications.

LESSON 22
SHARING DATA WITH OFFICE APPLICATIONS

In this lesson you learn to share data between Outlook and other Office applications.

CREATING A NEW OFFICE DOCUMENT

You can create a new Office document from within Outlook; for example, you can write a letter, write a report, or create a spreadsheet using any of the other Office 2000 applications. To create the document, you work in the actual Office application, such as Word, using that application's tools and features. When you save the document, a shortcut saves to Outlook so you can easily open the document at any time.

Outlook 2000 and Older Versions of Office Outlook 2000 has been designed to fully integrate with the applications in Microsoft Office 2000. You may lose functionality and have problems with the integration features if you use Outlook 2000 with an earlier version of Office.

To create a new Office document, follow these steps:

1. In the Outlook window, choose File, New, Office Document. The New Office Document dialog box appears, as shown in Figure 22.1.

I Don't See the New Document Dialog Box   In order for this dialog box to appear, Office must be installed and you must have at least one Office template located in the Microsoft Office Templates folder.

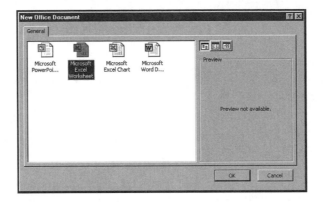

FIGURE 22.1   Select the template for your new Office document.

2. Select the template for an Excel worksheet or chart, a Word document, or a PowerPoint presentation, and click OK. Select one of the options in the dialog box that appears (either Post the Document in This Folder, meaning you want to save the file to your computer, or Send This Document to Someone, where an email message window opens and you build the document in that window). The template opens in a document (Excel, Word, or PowerPoint) window. Enter and format the text. Then use the menus to check spelling, create pictures, and otherwise manage the document as you would in a word processor, spreadsheet, or presentation software package.

3. To print the document, choose File, Print.

4. To save the document, choose File, Save As. The Save As dialog box appears.

5. Enter a filename and file type, and choose a location for the file.

6. Choose File, Close to close the document and the document window. The document is added to the Outlook item you were in when you created it.

To open the document for editing, printing, or other manipulation, double-click it.

CREATING AN OUTLOOK ITEM FROM AN OFFICE FILE

You can create an appointment from a Word document, a mail message from an Excel document, or one of many other items by dragging a file to an Outlook item. This capability is great for when you want to include data in a mail message or record items in your journal. Sharing data between Office applications makes your work easier and more efficient.

To create an Outlook item from an Office file, follow these steps:

1. Open the Windows Explorer window and the Outlook window so you can see both onscreen at the same time (see Figure 22.2). You can right click on the Windows taskbar and select Tile Windows Vertically or Tile Windows Horizontally to help you place the application windows on the desktop.

2. In the Explorer window, select the file from which you want to create an Outlook item, and then drag it to the folder in the Outlook bar. For example, drag a worksheet to the Tasks folder to create a task.

3. The New Item dialog box opens, with the Office file represented as an icon in the item. Enter any details, such as subject, dates, and so on, and then save the item as usual.

 Shortcut   Drag an Outlook item onto the Windows desktop to create a copy of the item that you can open quickly.

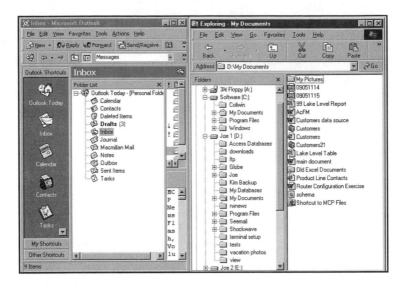

FIGURE 22.2   With two windows onscreen, you can drag items from one to the other.

IMPORTING AND EXPORTING FILES

You can import files to Outlook from other Office applications and export files from Outlook to other Office applications, such as Word and Excel. When you import, you're opening another Office application's file in a format that Outlook can read, so you can use the file's contents in Outlook. When you export, you're saving Outlook data in a format that one of the other Office applications can use.

IMPORTING

You can import files from Access, FoxPro, dBASE, Schedule+, Excel, or some other application for use in Outlook.

To import data, follow these steps:

1. In Outlook, choose File, Import and Export. The Import and Export Wizard appears (see Figure 22.3).

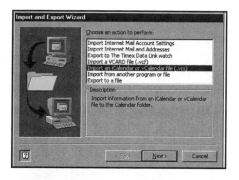

FIGURE 22.3   Import files to use in Outlook.

    Wizard   In Microsoft Office products, a Wizard is a series of dialog boxes containing instructions and options. A Wizard helps you complete a task.

2. Choose Import from Schedule+ or Another Program or File and click the Next button. The second Wizard dialog box appears.

3. Scroll through the list using the vertical scrollbar if necessary, and choose the type of file you want to import from the list. Click the Next button.

    Word's Not There!   You won't see Microsoft Word on the list, but you can still import a Word file. Select the Comma Separated Values (Windows) option to import a Word file that you've converted to text-only; first you'll have to use Word to save the Word file in Text Only format. If you are using Microsoft Word as your email editor in Outlook, you can open Word files directly; therefore, Outlook does not include Word on the Import list.

4. In the third Wizard dialog box, either enter the path and the filename in the File to Import text box or click the Browse button
and select the file from the Browse dialog box. Set any options
in the Options area of the dialog box, and click the Next button.

5. In the fourth Wizard dialog box, select the folder in which you
want to import the file, and click Next.

You may wonder why you should go through the import process when
you can drag a Word or Excel file into any of the Outlook items.
Importing a file translates the imported information into a format that
Outlook can use directly. For instance, information imported into a contact or task becomes the same as information you entered directly into the
contact or task. When you drag files onto Outlook items, you are embedding the file in the Outlook item, but you are not converting it. An Excel
workbook dragged into the Task Folder is embedded, which means a copy
of the workbook becomes a part of the Outlook item. When you double-
click an embedded object, such as an Excel workbook, the Outlook menus
and toolbars change to those found in Excel, enabling you to use Excel's
features as you work with the embedded object. (For more information
about Object Linking and Embedding, see "Linking and Embedding
Objects" later in this lesson.)

EXPORTING

You can export Outlook files to Access, Excel, Word, and so on for use
with other applications. For example, you might export an email message
to Word as a memo, or you might export data from your journal into an
Excel worksheet. When you export a file, you're saving the file's contents
in a format another application can open and use.

To export a file, follow these steps:

1. Select the item you want to export as a file and choose File,
Import and Export. The Import and Export Wizard appears.

2. Choose Export to a File and click Next.

3. In the second Wizard dialog box, select the folder to export from
and click Next.

4. In the third Wizard dialog box, select the file type and click Next.

5. In the fourth Wizard dialog box, enter the path and name of the file to be exported and then click Next.

LINKING AND EMBEDDING OBJECTS

You can use Windows OLE to share data between Office applications. Object Linking and Embedding is a feature that most Windows applications support. OLE enables you to share data between a source application and a destination application, ensuring that all documents are updated automatically and in a timely fashion. For example, you can link an Excel worksheet to a mail message to ensure that the data you send with the message is up-to-date and accurate. You also can embed objects into mail messages in Outlook.

One of the biggest advantages of using OLE is that you can edit an object by double-clicking it. When you do, the file is updated in both the source and the destination applications with the changes you've made. You can use existing files or create new files for both linking and embedding.

 Linking Creating a bridge between two applications so that the data in one application is copied exactly into the second application and updated automatically whenever changes are made.

Embedding Using one application to create an object within another application.

Source The application or document in which the object was created.

Destination The application or document into which the object is copied or embedded.

Object The Word document, Excel worksheet, Outlook Note, or other item that is linked or embedded.

LINKING OBJECTS

Outlook enables you to link data between two or more applications when you want to ensure that all data is kept up-to-date automatically. If, for example, you link an Excel worksheet to an Outlook message, each time you make a change to the numbers in the worksheet, those numbers also change in the linked data in the message.

 Linked Files Cannot Be Moved   When you create a link between a file, such as an Excel workbook, and an Outlook item, the link remains in force only as long as the Excel workbook remains in the same location on your computer. For example, if the Excel workbook is in an Excel folder on your computer's C: drive, the file must remain in this location if the link with the Outlook item is going to work.

To link an object between Outlook and another application, follow these steps:

1. In Outlook, create a new mail message or reply, and then place the insertion point in the body of the message.

2. Choose Insert, Object. The Object dialog box appears.

3. Choose Create from File. The Object dialog box changes to look like the one shown in Figure 22.4.

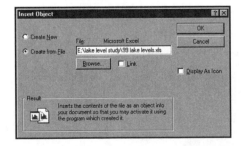

FIGURE 22.4   Create a link to an existing object.

4. Enter the path and filename of the object you want to link in the File text box, or click the Browse button and select the file.

5. Select the Link check box and click OK. Outlook inserts a copy of the object in the message text. The link remains—guaranteeing updated information—until you send the message.

EMBEDDING OBJECTS

You might want to embed a new or existing file, such as a Word table and text, into an email message to send to someone in your company. When you embed the data, the recipient can just double-click the embedded object to open, read, edit, and/or print the file's contents. Note, however, that embedded data (unlike linked data) isn't updated when a source file changes.

To embed an object in Outlook, follow these steps:

1. In Outlook, create a new mail message or reply, and then place the insertion point in the body of the message.

2. Choose Insert, Object. The Object dialog box appears.

3. Choose Create New, and a list of available Object Types appears in the dialog box.

4. Select the object type you want and click OK. Windows inserts a window into the message, from which you can create a document, spreadsheet, chart, or other object.

For example, if you choose to insert a spreadsheet, Windows creates a window within the message that looks like an Excel worksheet. In addition, the Outlook message window changes temporarily to look similar to Excel's, as shown in Figure 22.5.

Excel commands on the menus   Frame

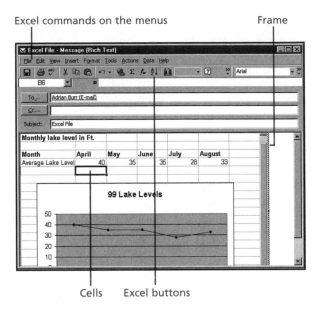

Cells   Excel buttons

FIGURE 22.5   Create a worksheet from within an Outlook message.

When you finish entering data, click outside the frame to return to Outlook. At any time, you can double-click anywhere in the frame to edit the data.

 Why the Entire Excel Workbook?   If you create an object from an existing Excel workbook, Outlook inserts the whole workbook into the item. You can display only one worksheet at a time, however. Double-click the Excel object to choose a different worksheet.

In this lesson you learned to share data between Outlook and other Office applications. In the next lesson you learn to archive items.

LESSON 23

ARCHIVING ITEMS

In this lesson you learn to use AutoArchive and to archive files, retrieve archived files, and delete archived files.

USING AUTOARCHIVE

You can set an option in Outlook to automatically archive your mail messages into files periodically. The AutoArchive feature cleans your Inbox for you but saves the specified messages in an archive file. AutoArchiving is very similar to the "backup" procedure that you use to compress and save files in case your computer crashes and you have to resort to disaster recovery. Mail messages are compressed and saved in a file that can then be transferred to a storage device such as a diskette or other removable drive (for example, an Iomega Zip drive or Imation Superdisk) for safekeeping.

 Archive To save items to a file that you can open at any time and print, view, or otherwise use. You might, for example, want to archive some of your mail messages to keep for your records instead of leaving those messages in your Inbox. Items that you select to archive are removed (deleted) from the folder that they resided in and are placed in an archive file.

To use AutoArchive, follow these steps:

1. Choose Tools, Options. The Options dialog box appears.

2. Click the Other tab.

3. Click the AutoArchive button to display the AutoArchive options (see Figure 23.1).

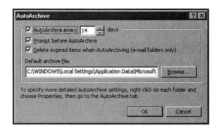

FIGURE **23.1**   Specify options for automatically archiving items into files.

4. Choose from the following check box options:

   AutoArchive Every *x* Days   Enter a number for how often (in days) you want Outlook to automatically archive items. If you enter **14**, for example, when you start Outlook on the 14th day, it automatically archives the contents of your folders into an archive file.

   Prompt Before AutoArchive   If you check this, Outlook displays a dialog box each time it is about to perform the AutoArchive; you can click OK or Cancel to continue or stop the operation.

   Delete Expired Items When AutoArchiving (E-Mail Folders Only)   Check this box to have Outlook remove messages from the Inbox and place them in the Deleted Items folder. These items are not included in the Archive file.

5. In the Default Archive File text box, enter a path to where you want to save the file, and name the archive file (if you don't want to use the default).

6. Click OK to close the AutoArchive dialog box. Click OK to close the Options dialog box.

In addition to setting the AutoArchive options in the AutoArchive dialog box, you can set additional AutoArchive options for each folder—Inbox, Tasks, Calendar, and so on. To set an individual folder's AutoArchive options, follow these steps:

1. Right-click the folder in the Outlook bar to display the shortcut menu.

2. Choose Properties. The item's Properties dialog box appears.

3. Choose the AutoArchive tab. Figure 23.2 shows the Inbox's AutoArchive tab.

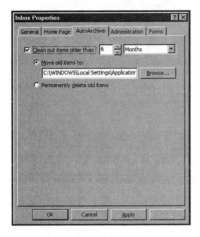

FIGURE **23.2** Set AutoArchive options for individual folders.

4. Set the options you want in the dialog box. You can choose to have old items (you set the time frame) cleaned out of the specific folder (they are deleted; select the Clean Out Items check box) or you can set the location where old items will be moved to (select the Move Old Items To radio button and then specify a folder).

5. Click OK to close the dialog box.

ARCHIVING MANUALLY

You can choose to archive one or two folders or all folders manually whenever you're ready to create an archive file. If you choose to do it yourself, you control exactly how and when archives are created.

To create an archive, follow these steps:

1. Choose File, Archive. The Archive dialog box appears (see Figure 23.3).

FIGURE 23.3   Enter settings for manual archiving.

2. Choose one of the following options:

   Archive All Folders According to Their AutoArchive Settings
   Use this option to save archives of each folder, using the settings you select in the AutoArchive tab of the folder's Properties dialog box.

   Archive This Folder and All Subfolders   Select this option to archive the selected folder.

3. Either enter a date in the Archive Items Older Than text box or select a date from the drop-down calendar.

4. In the Archive File text box, enter a path and filename with which to save the file.

5. Click OK to archive the selected folder(s).

RETRIEVING ARCHIVED FILES

You can retrieve an archived file by importing it. When you retrieve an archived file, it becomes a part of your Outlook folder just as it was before you archived it. Outlook archived files (.PST files) are saved in a special format and can only be opened using Outlook.

To retrieve an archived file, follow these steps:

1. Choose File, Import and Export. The Import and Export Wizard dialog box appears.

2. Choose Import from Another File or Program and then click Next.

3. In the Import a File dialog box, select Personal Folders File (*.PST) and click the Next button.

4. In the Import Personal Folders dialog box, enter the path and the filename of the archived file. Select any one of the following options:

    Replace Duplicates with Items Imported   Copies of the data will be overwritten by imported items.

    Allow Duplicates to Be Created   Imported items will not overwrite copies but will create duplicates of those items.

    Do Not Import Duplicates   This option preserves the originals in the folder instead of overwriting them with items from the archived file.

    Click the Next button.

5. In the Choose Folders dialog box of the Import/Export Wizard, choose the folder into which you want to import. (The default is to import the archived item to the Personal Folders area; you may have created subfolders into which you want to import.)

DELETING ARCHIVED FILES

The easiest way to delete archived files is by using the Windows Explorer. However, you can also delete files from the Find Files and Folders dialog box or from My Computer (both part of Windows).

To delete an archived file, follow these steps:

1. Open Windows Explorer and locate the files. Archived files are saved with a .PST extension in the My Documents folder (by default) or any other folder you designate.

2. Open the folder containing the files and select the file(s) you want to delete.

3. Press the Delete key, or drag the file(s) to the Recycle Bin.

4. Empty the Recycle Bin by right-clicking the Bin and choosing Empty Recycle Bin.

5. Close Explorer by clicking the Close (X) button.

In this lesson you learned to use AutoArchive and to archive files, retrieve archived files, and delete archived files. In the next lesson you learn to customize Outlook.

LESSON 24

CUSTOMIZING OUTLOOK

In this lesson you learn to set email, calendar, and other options in Outlook.

SETTING OUTLOOK OPTIONS

You can set all of Outlook's options by using the Options dialog box. (To open the Options dialog box, select Tools, Options.) The number of tabs on this dialog box will depend on the installation option you chose when you installed Outlook (Internet E-mail Only or Corporate installation). The Options dialog box for the Corporate configuration can have eight tabs: Preferences, Mail Services, Mail Format, Spelling, Security, Other, Delegates, and Internet E-mail (depending on the services you have set up). Each of the tabs controls a specific category of Outlook's settings. For example, the Other tab of the Options dialog box, shown in Figure 24.1, controls options such as Deleted Items Folder, AutoArchive, and Preview Pane.

You will find that the tabs available in the Options dialog box for the Internet Only installation of Outlook reflect that fact that only one kind of email service is available: Internet email. Also, because you work with accounts rather than services in the Internet Only installation, the Mail delivery tab enables you to quickly access the Accounts Manager (see Figure 24.2).

FIGURE **24.1**   The Options dialog box gives you control over all the features of Outlook 2000.

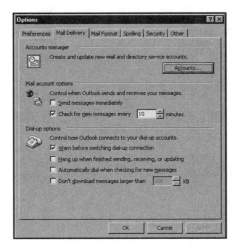

FIGURE **24.2**   The Options dialog box tabs will be different for Outlook when you use the Internet E-mail Only configuration.

Each tab in the Options dialog box has some obvious settings that you can control with radio buttons or check boxes. Each tab also contains buttons that enable you to set more specific options.

SETTING EMAIL OPTIONS

E-mail, Calendar, Tasks, Contacts, and Notes options are set on the Preferences tab of the Options dialog box. To open a more specific dialog box related to the features of each of the Outlook item types, click the appropriate button on the Preferences tab (see Figure 24.3).

FIGURE 24.3   Customize Email, Calendar, Tasks, Contacts, and Notes options on the Preferences tab.

To set email options, follow these steps:

1. On the Preferences tab, click the E-mail Options button.

2. The E-mail Options dialog box appears. This dialog box enables you to set items using check boxes and drop-down menus; there are also buttons for Advanced E-mail Options and Tracking Options.

3. In the Message Handling box of the E-mail Options dialog box, check the boxes of the options you want to activate, such as Close Original Message on Reply or Forward or Save Copies of Messages in Sent Items Folder.

4. Two drop-down boxes in the On Replies and Forwards section provide you with options for replying to and forwarding messages. You can choose whether or not you want to include the original message text with replies and forwards, or whether to attach the original message as an attached file.

5. You can also set Advanced E-mail options and Tracking options in this dialog box. When you click the Advanced E-mail Options button, the Advanced E-mail Options dialog box appears. This dialog box enables you to control how unsent messages are handled, what happens when new mail arrives, and the importance level of new messages that you send. When you've completed setting options in this dialog box, click OK.

6. The Tracking Options button in the E-mail Options dialog box opens the Tracking Options dialog box. In this box you can set options that notify you when email you send is received and when that email is read. After setting options in this dialog box, click OK. Click OK again to close the E-mail Options dialog box.

SETTING CALENDAR OPTIONS

If you work unusual days or hours, you can change your default Calendar workweek in the Calendar Options dialog box. Suppose your workweek runs from Tuesday through Saturday, and your workday is from 4 a.m. to noon. You can make changes to the Calendar so that it reflects your actual workweek. You also can set your time zone and add holidays to your calendar. To open the Calendar Options dialog box, click the Calendar Options button on the Preferences tab of the Options dialog box.

Follow these steps to make changes to the Calendar Options (see Figure 24.4):

1. In the Calendar Working Week area, set your starting and ending time. (The default is 8 a.m. to 5 p.m.)

2. To set the time zone for your area, click the Time Zone button, and then choose the zone that includes your location.

3. To add holidays to your calendar, click the Add Holidays button. Check the box representing your country (U.S. is the default) and click OK. Outlook imports the U.S. holidays to the calendar.

4. When you finish setting the options in this dialog box, return to the Preferences tab by clicking OK.

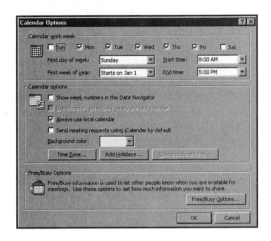

FIGURE 24.4 Customize your Calendar in the Calendar Options dialog box.

The Preferences tab also enables you to set options for your other Outlook items, such as Tasks, Contacts, and Notes.

SETTING MAIL SERVICES AND MAIL FORMAT OPTIONS

The Mail Services tab enables you to set options that govern which Outlook Profile is loaded when Outlook starts and which of your installed mail services is checked for mail. Click the appropriate check boxes for the services you want selected when new messages, such as faxes and email, are downloaded to your Inbox.

If you installed Outlook for Internet Only, Outlook does not need a profile to load the services that you install such as your Internet email account and Outlook Fax. For more information on the Internet Only and Corporate email installations, see Lesson 3, "Understanding the Outlook Configurations."

 Profile   A group of settings that control how your mail is delivered, received, and stored in Outlook, and the software used to transfer your mail, such as Microsoft Mail, Microsoft Exchange, Lotus Notes, and so on.

 Check for New Mail?   Mail types listed in the Check for New Mail On list box are added when you add new profiles to Outlook. You add a profile by choosing Tools, Services.

The Mail Format tab in the Options dialog box enables you to choose your Message format, such as HTML, Plain Text, Microsoft Word, and Microsoft Exchange Rich Text. The Mail format that you use will dictate the special fonts and WordMail templates that are available to you. Remember, however, that special fonts and templates will be of no use to you if those receiving your messages do not have email software that can take advantage of the fonts and formatting. To always send plain text to certain individuals, open their Properties dialog box in the Address book and click the Send E-mail Using Plain Text only check box.

 Applying Your Changes   When you make changes on the tabs of the Options dialog box, apply these new options to Outlook by clicking the Apply button. The Options dialog box remains open so that you can configure other options.

OTHER OPTIONS DIALOG BOX TABS

The Options dialog box contains additional tabs that control other features associated with Outlook. The tabs are listed here with a description of the settings available.

Spelling This tab enables you to change settings associated with Outlook's spell checker. You can choose (using check boxes) to have the speller always suggest replacements for misspelled words, always check spelling before sending, and ignore words in uppercase. A drop-down box also enables you to pick the language of the dictionary you want to use to spell check your Outlook items.

Internet E-mail This tab enables you to set the coding scheme for Internet email attachments. There is also a setting that will have Outlook periodically check your network for new email messages. This tab will only appear when you use the Outlook Corporate E-mail configuration.

Security This tab enables you to set options regarding whether or not outgoing messages should be encrypted or have digital signatures attached to them. There is also an option that enables you to get a digital ID to use for your outgoing messages.

When you have completed all the changes you want to make to the various Outlook options, click OK to close the Options dialog box.

In this lesson you learned to set email, calendar, and other options in Outlook. In the next lesson you learn to send and receive faxes using Outlook.

LESSON 25
MANAGING FAXES WITH OUTLOOK

In this lesson you learn how to set up and use the Windows Fax and Symantec's WinFax services in Outlook and to send, receive, and manage faxes.

SETTING UP THE FAX SERVICE

Microsoft Outlook can be used to send and receive faxes using Microsoft Fax. To use Microsoft Fax when you are in Outlook, you must configure its features so that your computer can send or receive faxes over a modem or a network that uses a network fax server.

Microsoft Fax is only available if you are using the Corporate installation of Microsoft Outlook. If you are using the Internet Only configuration of Outlook, you can send and receive faxes using Symantec's WinFax Starter Edition, which is installed with Outlook for Internet Only. For more about this alternative method of sending and receiving faxes, see "Using WinFax" later in this lesson.

Adding the Microsoft Fax service to Outlook is very straightforward if you installed Outlook in the Corporate configuration. New services such as Microsoft Fax are added via the Outlook Tools menu. To add a new service to Outlook, follow these steps:

1. In the Outlook window click the Tools menu and then click Services. The Services dialog box appears (see Figure 25.1).

Installing Microsoft Fax in Windows 98 Microsoft Fax is not a standard communication component of Windows 98 as it was in Windows 95 (where it was an installation option). After you install Windows 98, you will have to manually install the Microsoft Fax software to your computer. Make sure the Windows 98 CD is in your CD-ROM drive. Click the Start button and then click Run. In the Run dialog box, type E:\tools\oldwin95\message\us\awfax (E: would be the letter of your CD-ROM drive). Then click OK. The Microsoft Fax software will be installed on your computer. Make sure that you install the Microsoft Fax software before you install Outlook.

FIGURE **25.1** The Services dialog box enables you to add, remove, and control the properties of the services included in your Outlook User Profile.

2. Click the Add button to add a new service.

3. The Add Service to Profile dialog box appears. All the available services such as Microsoft Fax will be listed in this box.

4. To add Microsoft Fax to the Outlook services, select Microsoft Fax, then click OK.

No Fax Service If you attempt to add the Microsoft Fax service and it is not available in the Services dialog box, you have installed Outlook in the Internet Only configuration. You can choose to uninstall Outlook using the Add/Remove Programs icon in the Windows Control Panel and then reinstall Outlook in the Corporate configuration.

5. A Microsoft Fax message box appears letting you know that you must provide certain information (such as your name, fax number, and modem type) before you can send and receive faxes in Outlook. Click Yes to continue.

6. The Microsoft Fax Properties dialog box appears (see Figure 25.2). This dialog box is where you supply the information that Outlook needs to send and receive faxes via Microsoft Fax.

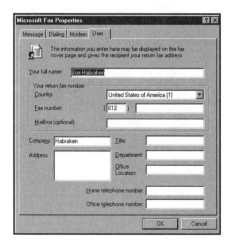

FIGURE 25.2 The Microsoft Fax Properties dialog box is where you supply Outlook with the information that it needs to send and receive faxes using Microsoft Fax.

Here is a brief description of the tab contents:

User   The User tab is where you provide information about yourself. This information includes your name and your return fax number and information regarding the company you work for. Much of the information is optional; however, you must provide your name and a return fax number on this tab.

Modem   The Modem tab provides a list of the modems currently installed on your PC. Select the modem you want to use to send and receive your faxes.

Dialing   The Dialing tab enables you to set the number of retries the modem will make when dialing a fax number. This tab also gives you access to other dialing properties such as dialing to access an outside line or using a calling card when dialing.

Message   The Message tab is where you select the time to send the fax, the type of cover page to use when sending, and the page format used for the message.

You must fill out the information on the User tab and select a modem to send and receive your faxes on the Modem tab. After you have done this, click OK. The Microsoft Fax service appears in your Services dialog box. Click OK to close it.

You may get a message that the new service you added (such as Microsoft Fax) will not operate until the next time you start Outlook. If this is the case, close Outlook and restart the program, so that the Fax service is available.

 Accessing Properties   If you chose to close the Microsoft Fax Properties box after you added the Fax service to Outlook, you can reopen the properties box via the Tools menu. Click Tools, Microsoft Fax Tools, and then select Options.

SENDING FAXES

After you've configured Microsoft Fax, you are ready to send faxes using Microsoft Outlook. New faxes are launched via the Outlook Compose menu. To create a new fax, follow these steps:

1. Click the Actions menu, then click New Fax. The Compose New Fax Wizard appears.

2. You must specify your dialing location (which is usually the default setting unless you are using a portable computer) using the drop-down box in the Wizard window. Click Next to continue.

 Skip a Screen   If you are not using a portable computer you can remove the opening screen from the Compose New Fax Wizard so it won't appear in the future. Click the "I'm Not Using a Portable Computer, So Don't Show This to Me Again" check box.

3. The next screen is where you enter the information pertaining to the person to whom you want to send the fax. Type the person's name in the To: box. Select the country that you are sending the fax to using the drop-down Country box. Type the fax number in the Fax # box (see Figure 25.3).

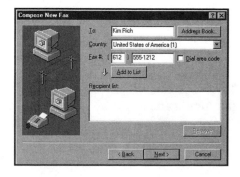

FIGURE 25.3   Enter the recipient's name and fax number in the appropriate boxes.

Use Address Book   You can also enter the name of the person you are sending the fax to using your Outlook Address Book or Contacts list. Click the Address Book button and then double-click the name or names to add to the list. Make sure that you have included each person's fax number in his address book entry before using this method of selecting names for the fax.

4. After completing the entries, click Add to List. The person's name will be added to the recipient box. Repeat the procedure for any other people you want to send the fax to, then click Next.

5. The next screen enables you to select a cover page style for your fax; click the appropriate radio button to select your fax cover page style. If you don't want a fax cover page, click the No radio button.

6. On the next screen type the subject of your fax in the Subject box. If you want to include a note on the cover sheet, type it in the Note box.

7. Once you've completed your note, click the Next button to continue. The next screen is where you designate the body of your fax message. You can attach a document, spreadsheet, or other file type to a fax in Outlook. The added file will serve as the pages of the fax and be included with your fax cover page.

8. Click Add File to browse your hard drive, select the file, and click Open to add the file to the fax and return to the Fax Wizard. Click Next to continue.

9. When you've completed the fax composition and are ready to send the fax, click Finish. The Microsoft Fax Status box appears.

10. The fax is formatted to be sent and the phone number you specified is dialed. Once a connection is made your fax is sent and the Fax Status window appears, keeping you apprised of the status of the sending fax. When the fax is sent the Status box disappears.

Troubleshooting the Configuration   If Microsoft Fax does not access the modem correctly and your fax is aborted, you may need to troubleshoot the configuration that you've set up to send and receive faxes. From the Help menu select Microsoft Help Topics. Under Contents, double-click the Troubleshooting icon. The help system walks you through your fax and modem setup to try to help you fix any problems.

RECEIVING AND PROCESSING FAXES

The faxes that you receive will eventually be available in the Outlook Inbox. How Microsoft Fax answers the call for an incoming fax depends on whether you are using a modem with its own line or if you share one line between your phone and modem.

If your modem has its own line, you can set it to automatically answer incoming fax calls. Follow these steps:

1. Click Tools, then point at Microsoft Fax Tools; click Options to open to Microsoft Fax Properties box. Select the Modem tab.

2. To set the fax properties of the modem, click Properties. The Fax Modem Properties box appears.

3. To set the answer mode to automatic, click the Answer After radio dial and then set the number of rings you want to wait until the modem answers the incoming fax call.

4. You also can set the modem speaker volume in this box by dragging the speaker volume switch. After setting your answer options and speaker volume, click OK. You will be returned to the Microsoft Fax Options box. Click OK to close it.

To receive a fax manually you need to know that the incoming call on your phone line is a fax rather than voice call. You should verify with the sender when he plans to send the fax to you, so that you can manually answer the fax call using Microsoft Fax.

When you open Microsoft Outlook, a fax machine icon is placed on the right side of the Windows taskbar. This icon supplies you with the tool to answer your fax calls.

1. Click the fax machine icon on the taskbar. The Microsoft Fax Status box opens.

2. When your telephone rings, click the Answer Now button on the Microsoft Fax Status box.

3. Microsoft Fax directs your modem to answer the incoming call. The Idle designator on the Microsoft Fax Status box changes to "Answering Call."

4. After the connection is established, the Status box displays the status of each page of the fax as it is received.

5. When the fax transmission is complete, the Fax Status box returns to "Idle." Click the Close button to close the status box.

After you've received a fax, either by having your modem answer the call automatically, or by answering the call manually, you need to download the received fax to Microsoft Outlook. Once the fax is in the Outlook Inbox, you can read it, print it, or move it to another Inbox folder.

To download the new fax to the Outlook Inbox, choose Send and Receive from the Outlook Tools menu. New faxes and email will be downloaded into your Inbox.

READING FAXES

Opening a new fax in the Outlook Inbox is handled in the same way that you read the other items that appear in your Inbox such as your new email messages. To open a new fax, follow these steps:

1. In the Outlook Inbox double-click the fax message you want to read. A fax viewer window opens displaying the fax, as shown in Figure 25.4.

Print button   Zoom In   Zoom Out

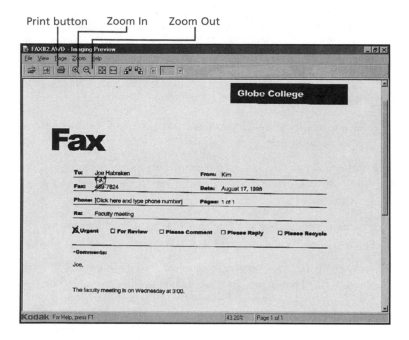

FIGURE 25.4   You can read the faxes that you receive in the viewer window.

2. The Fax Viewer enables you to zoom in (or out) on the fax to get a better view. Click the Zoom In button on the viewer toolbar. Zoom in on the fax until you can easily read the text.

3. If you would like a hard copy of the fax, click the Print button. The file version of the fax will be formatted and printed as a facsimile of the original document.

4. When you have completed viewing or printing your fax, close the Fax Viewer. You will be returned to the Outlook Inbox.

You can delete, move, or copy faxes in your Inboxes just as you would email messages.

USING WINFAX

When you install Outlook using the Internet E-mail Only option, you can still send and receive faxes using WinFax. This fax utility is installed as one of the Internet accounts found in the Accounts dialog box.

To view the WinFax account, select the Tools menu, then select Accounts. Your current email account and the WinFax account will appear in the Internet Accounts dialog box, as shown in Figure 25.5.

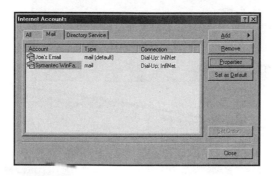

FIGURE 25.5   The Accounts dialog box enables you to set the parameters for the WinFax service.

You should not tamper with any of the Properties settings for the WinFax account; these are set for you during the Outlook installation. Click the Close button to close the Internet Accounts dialog box.

To set the options for the WinFax account, open the Tools menu, then choose Options. Select the Fax tab in the Options dialog box. The Fax tab enables you to set your Fax number, select a cover page for the faxes you send using WinFax, and select the modem that you will use to send and receive your faxes.

Before closing the Fax options, you may want to click the Automatic Receive Fax check box in the dialog box. This sets WinFax to automatically answer your phone using the modem after the number of rings you specify. Once you have set the options for the Fax account, click OK.

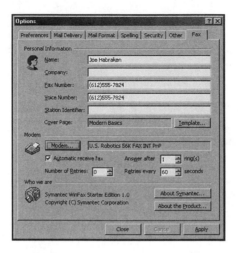

FIGURE 25.6   Set the options for your WinFax account on the Fax tab of the Options dialog box.

    Select a Modem for WinFax   If a modem does not appear in the Modem box on the Fax tab, click the Modem button. The Modem Properties dialog box appears. If a modem is available in this dialog box, click the modem and select Properties. The WinFax wizard will set up your modem for the WinFax account. If a modem does not appear in the Modem Properties dialog box, select Add and a search will be made to find your modem. Once the modem is found, click the Properties button and the WinFax wizard will set up your modem for use with the Fax account.

Sending a fax with the WinFax account is a little different from sending a fax with Microsoft Fax. To send a fax using WinFax, follow these steps:

1. Select File, then point at New and select Fax Message. The new fax message appears in a message window (see Figure 25.7).

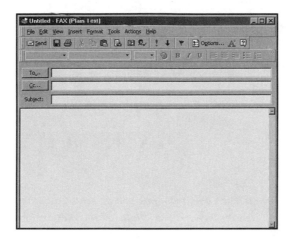

FIGURE 25.7   The blank fax message appears.

2. Select a recipient for the fax by clicking the To button and then
    selecting the recipient from your Address Book or Contact
    folder. The selected contact must have a fax number entered in
    his contact information, so that WinFax knows the appropriate
    fax number for the recipient.

3. After selecting the recipient, enter the subject and text for the
    fax.

4. Click the Send button to send your fax to the recipient.

You will find that WinFax does not have quite the number of bells and
whistles that Microsoft Fax possesses, so when your fax is sent it appears
that you are sending typical email. A separate fax status box will not
appear on the Windows desktop.

In this lesson you learned how to set up the Outlook Fax service and send
and receive faxes using Microsoft Fax and WinFax. In the next lesson you
learn how to take advantage of Internet services such as Newsgroups from
within Outlook.

LESSON 26

OUTLOOK 2000
AND THE
INTERNET

In this lesson you learn about Outlook and its connection to the Internet, using Outlook Express Newsreader, Microsoft Internet Explorer, and Microsoft NetMeeting. You also learn how to use Net Folders.

USING NEWSGROUPS

Microsoft Outlook not only provides all the tools you need to manage your messages, contacts, and calendar, but it also provides you with an easy connection to Internet services, such as newsgroups and the World Wide Web. Outlook even enables you to conduct real-time meetings over the Internet.

Newsgroups are a large collection of discussion groups held on news servers around the world. A particular newsgroup is much like a bulletin board; you can read messages posted there and post your own. Newsgroups cover information from current events to software, hobbies, pets, and other personal interests.

 Newsgroup An Internet online bulletin board that enables users to post and read messages. Newsgroups are part of Usenet, which is a consortium of Internet news servers that enable users such as yourself to download and post messages.

To access Internet newsgroups and read or reply to the postings there, you need a newsreader. When you install Microsoft Outlook, the Microsoft Outlook Express newsreader software is also installed. (There are a number of newsreaders available for use on the Internet and some are integrated with Web browsers, such as Outlook Express.)

SETTING UP THE NEWSREADER

You can access newsgroups from Outlook by starting the Outlook Express Newsreader. First you must make sure that you are connected to the Internet through your corporate network or by your dial-up connection to your Internet service provider. After you've connected, follow these steps to start the Outlook Express Newsreader and download newsgroup postings.

1. In the Outlook window, select News from the Go menu. The Outlook Express Newsreader opens.

2. The first time you use the Newsreader, it runs the Internet Connection Wizard, which leads you through the process of setting up your news server and creating a newsgroup account for you (see Figure 26.1). The first screen asks you to type the name you will use when you post messages to your news server. After typing a name, click Next.

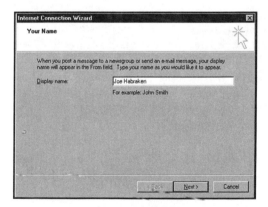

FIGURE 26.1   The Internet Connection Wizard walks you through the steps of setting up your news server.

3. The next screen asks you to provide your email address. Click Next after doing so.

4. On the next screen, you must provide the name of your news server. This name should be provided to you by your network administrator or Internet service provider. Click Next after entering the server name (it will be something like news.company.com).

5. The next screen asks you to type a friendly name for the new account. Type a name and then click Next.

6. The last screen asks you to select the type of connection you will use to access the Internet: your phone line, Local Area Network, or a manual connection. Select the connection type, and then click Next.

7. The last screen appears, letting you know you've completed the process. Click Finish.

 Friendly Names for Accounts   The friendly name that you choose for your new account in step 5 will appear on your Outlook Express folder list and can be used to open the newsgroups to which you subscribe. This account name differs from the name that you must choose in step 2, which actually identifies the postings that you place on the news server and is seen by everyone who looks at the posts in the newsgroup. You should choose your newsgroup posting name carefully. You don't want to inadvertently offend anyone when you post or have your posts be taken less seriously than you intend.

When you complete the account creation process, a message box appears telling you that the newsgroups available on your news server will be downloaded. After the newsgroups are downloaded, the Newsgroup Subscriptions dialog box for the news account appears (see Figure 26.2).

The Newsgroup Subscriptions dialog box enables you to "subscribe" to a particular newsgroup by selecting the newsgroup name and then clicking the Subscribe button. This will place the newsgroup on the Subscribed tab of the Newsgroup Subscriptions dialog box, making it easier for you to find and access a particular newsgroup.

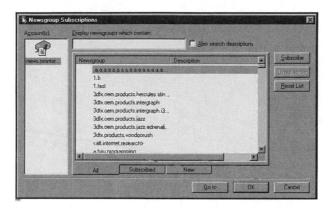

FIGURE 26.2   Use the Newsgroup Subscriptions dialog box to subscribe to newsgroups that you want to read and post to.

 Find Your Newsgroups   The Find box at the top of the Subscriptions dialog box enables you to quickly find newsgroups that contain a particular keyword. Type the word in the Find box and then click Find to search for all the newsgroups that contain your search word in their names.

After subscribing to the newsgroups you want to read, click OK. You return to the Outlook Express window (see Figure 26.3). A list of the groups you subscribed to appears in the News window on the right side of the Outlook Express Window.

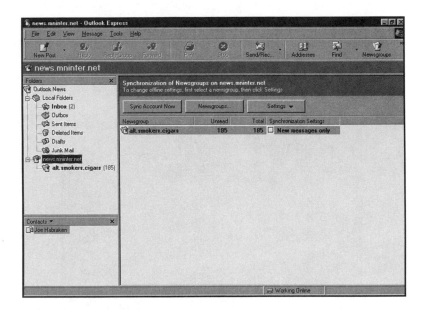

FIGURE 26.3 The Outlook Express Newsreader enables you to read and post messages in Internet newsgroups.

READING NEWSGROUP POSTINGS

After you have set up an account and downloaded and subscribed to newsgroups, you are ready to read and post messages. If you have just subscribed to your newsgroups for the first time and have closed the Newsgroup Subscriptions dialog box, just double-click any of your subscribed groups to read the postings.

In the future when you enter the Outlook Express window (via Outlook and the View menu) click Read News on the main Outlook Express window in the Newsgroups area of the window. Your newsgroups will appear as shown in Figure 26.3. Double-click any of your subscribed newsgroups to download and view the postings.

Messages in the newsgroup appear in the Message pane. To read a particular message, click the message. The message text appears in the preview pane (see Figure 26.4). You also can open a separate message window by double-clicking a particular posting.

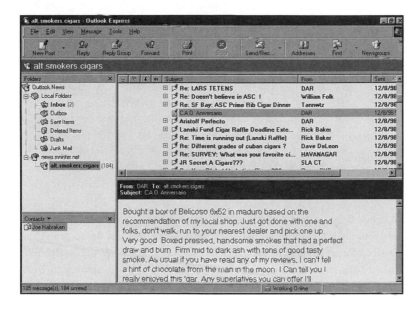

FIGURE 20.4   Select a message in the Newsgroup window to read it in the preview pane.

POSTING TO NEWSGROUPS

To post your own message to a newsgroup, you follow a procedure that is similar to sending new email messages using Outlook itself. In the Outlook Express window, select the newsgroup you want to post to.

Click the New Post button on the Outlook Express toolbar. A new message window opens. Type a subject for the message in the Subject box. Type the message itself in the message pane of the new message window. After you've completed your message, click the Send button.

A message window appears telling you that your new message has been posted but may not immediately appear with the messages already in the newsgroup.

When you have completed reading and sending newsgroup messages, you can close the Outlook Express Newsreader by clicking the Outlook Express Close (X) button. You will be returned to the Outlook 98 window.

Posting Etiquette   When you post to newsgroups, you should follow the same rules of politeness that you use when you converse with someone in person or by email. Do not type in all caps; this is considered shouting. Remember that humor and sarcasm are not always apparent in written communication. Be as straightforward and clear as you can in your postings. An extremely annoying post can lead to "flaming," or a barrage of angry and unsolicited email.

When you find a post that you want to respond to, or you want to send email to the individual who made the post, select the post message in the Outlook Express message window. Then either click the Reply to Group button (this sends a post in response to the selected post), or the Reply to Author button to send email to the author of the post.

 Unsubscribing from Newsgroups   If you want to unsubscribe from a newsgroup, click the Newsgroup button on the Outlook Express toolbar. In the Newsgroup Subscriptions dialog box, select the Subscribed tab. To remove a group from your subscription list, select the Newsgroup and then click the Unsubscribe button.

LAUNCHING INTERNET EXPLORER

You also can launch Microsoft Internet Explorer 5 from the Outlook window. This enables you to quickly browse the World Wide Web. Again, before launching Internet Explorer, you must be connected to the Internet either by your company network or by dial-up connection to your Internet service provider.

Launching Other Web Browsers If you use another Web browser, such as Netscape Navigator, you will not be able to launch it directly from Outlook. Create a shortcut for your browser on the desktop so that you can launch it quickly when you need it.

To start Internet Explorer, choose Web Browser from the Go menu. The Internet Explorer window opens (see Figure 26.5).

You can browse the Web using all the features of Internet Explorer. Use links on your home page to move to other Web pages, or click the Search button to find other sites of interest.

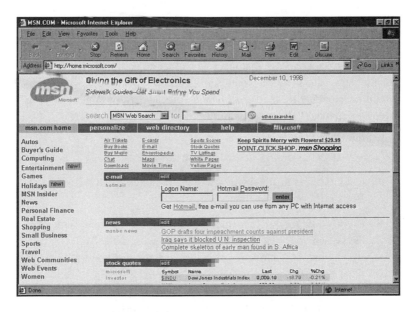

Figure 26.5 Internet Explorer provides you with all the capabilities you need to take advantage of the World Wide Web.

Launching Internet Explorer from Outlook Messages
You also can launch Internet Explorer from Outlook messages that contain Web page references. Web page addresses in your Outlook email messages appear in blue and serve as hyperlinks. Click the Web address in the message (such as **http://www.mcp.com**), and Internet Explorer will start and open the designated Web page.

When you have completed your use of Internet Explorer, click the Close (X) button in the Explorer window. You will be returned to the Outlook 98 window.

LAUNCHING MICROSOFT NETMEETING

Another software package that takes advantage of communication on the Internet and that can be launched from Outlook is Microsoft NetMeeting. Microsoft NetMeeting enables real-time voice and video communication over the Internet. This enables you to conduct "live" meetings without leaving your office.

To start NetMeeting from Outlook, follow these steps:

1. Click Go, and then point at Internet Call; click From Address Book or Start NetMeeting.

2. If you chose the Address Book option, double-click the name of the person you want to hold the meeting with in the Address Book window. NetMeeting will start and connect you to the other participant (skip to step 4). If you clicked Start NetMeeting, you will have to select the other participant from the list of users currently logged in to the NetMeeting server, as shown in Figure 26.6.

FIGURE 26.6 The NetMeeting server lists all individuals currently logged in to the various Microsoft NetMeeting communication servers.

 Launching NetMeeting from Outlook If you plan to launch NetMeeting sessions directly from the Address Book or your Contacts list, you must make sure that you have entered the contact's email address in the appropriate field. NetMeeting uses the email address to find the person on the NetMeeting Server that she is connected to.

3. Double-click the name of the person you want to meet with in the NetMeeting directory server list.

4. Regardless of which route you used to start the new meeting, the Current Call window opens. At this point you are connected to the other individual and can hold your meeting using audio and video (if the appropriate hardware is available on both users' computers). NetMeeting also provides a Chat window that the participants can use to communicate by typing (see Figure 26.7).

5. When you have completed your meeting, close the Current Call
   window, and then close the NetMeeting window. You will be
   returned to the Outlook 98 window.

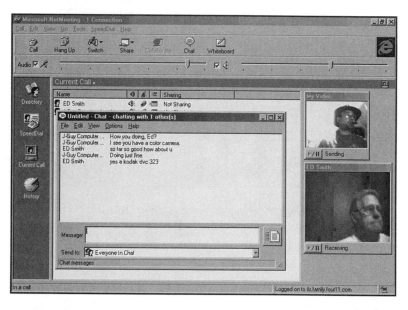

FIGURE 26.7   NetMeeting's Current Call window enables you to use
audio, video, and/or your keyboard to communicate with others.

 Launching NetMeeting from the Contacts Folder   You
also can launch NetMeeting conferences from your
Contacts folder. Open a Contact form for a particular
contact. From the Actions menu choose Call Using
NetMeeting. NetMeeting will be launched, and you
will be connected to the appropriate meeting server
and then to your contact.

WORKING WITH NET FOLDERS

Outlook provides a lot of team computing power when you use it in a corporate environment. You can share folders and create new folders that are available to everyone who has an account and the appropriate rights on a network. Outlook affords a great deal of flexibility for sharing information when you use the Corporate installation option and connect to a network using Microsoft Exchange Server.

Outlook does not leave those who use the Internet E-mail installation configuration and connect to the Internet using a service provider out in the cold, however. You can share Contact and Calendar information and create shared folders that can be accessed over the Internet by other users. These folders are called Net Folders.

You can publish a Net Folder or subscribe to a Net Folder that has been published by someone else. Net Folders can be based on any of the folders in Outlook except your Inbox or Outbox.

To create a Net Folder based on an Outlook item such as your Calendar, follow these steps.

1. Select the File menu, then select Share. Select Calendar on the cascading menu that appears (or any of the other items listed).

2. The Net Folder Wizard appears. The opening screen says "Sharing Your Calendar" (or names any other folder item you selected to share). To begin the sharing process, click the Next button.

3. The next screen asks you to select contacts from your Personal Address Book or Outlook Contacts list with whom you want to share the file. Select a name on the left side of the dialog box and then click the To button to include that person in the Subscriber Database.

4. When you have completed your selection of Subscribers, click OK. The next Net Folder Wizard screen shows a list of the subscribers for the Net Folder. Click Next to continue.

5. On the next screen, enter a description for the shared folder, such as **This is Joe's Calendar** or some other name that will easily identify the shared folder. Click Next to move to the final screen in the Net Folder creation process, and then click Finish.

You now have a shared folder that appears in your Outlook folder list. When you complete the Net Folder creation process using the Net Folder Wizard, invitations are automatically sent out to all the email addresses that appear in the Subscribers list you created. If a Subscriber accepts the invitation to share your new Net Folder, the new folder will also appear on his list of Outlook folders.

You also can share Net Folders created by others by accepting an invitation to share a Net Folder. You receive the invitation as an email message in your Inbox. Simply click the Accept button at the bottom of the invitation, and a copy of the Net Folder is placed in your folder list.

In this lesson, you learned how to read newsgroup postings using the Microsoft Outlook Express Newsreader. You learned to launch Internet Explorer from the Outlook window and to launch meetings on the Internet using Microsoft NetMeeting. You also learned how to create and share a Net Folder.

INDEX

T

W-Z